✶ ✶ ✶ ✶ ✶ ✶ ✶ ✶

"This book holds a t just children but the adults in their lives. It would have meant the world to me to have a book like this when I was a frightened, isolated child. I am so grateful and happy to think that young people are being supported, heard, and seen in the modern world by writers like Margaret Rooke."
Andi Oliver, chef, broadcaster

"As this book shows, being different can almost certainly bring its own challenges but it can also develop strengths, genuine friendships, and often lots of fun! Celebrate everything that makes you smile, makes you laugh, and brings you joy. Surround yourselves with loved ones and never hang about with anyone that tries to clip your wings!"
Diane Carson, star of *Traitors UK* (series 2), former youth worker and teacher

"This is a wonderful book. The simple but effective storytelling helps to get across important information about differences, some obvious, some not so obvious, in a world that's increasingly about the 'shop window'."
Annalisa Barbieri, columnist, *The Guardian*

"One person who really stood out to me was Sarah, 14, in Ireland. She takes care of her younger sister, Esther, who has Down Syndrome and other complex medical needs. It reminds me of my brother, Cruz. He also has medical needs and requires help. So this part in the book made me realize I'm not alone."
Sawyer, 10, Maryland, USA

✶ ✶

✶ ✶

"Margaret Rooke spans the globe as she gives the reader a lens through which to view our beautifully diverse world. Rooke also provides the storytellers with a vehicle to express not only their stories, but their teachings, lessons learned, and advice to all on the importance of acceptance and tolerance. *Different Like Us!* allows children to learn from one another. It gives a child-centred and honest perspective on the diverse world that we live in and is an ideal resource for all classrooms and homes."
Adam Barrett, primary school teacher, Cork, Ireland

"This book is a very safe space that helps people realize that not everybody's the same. It helps people feel welcome and know that even though they feel different, they belong."
Elsa, 10, Washington DC, USA

"This book is a powerful reminder that every child's experience in school is unique. The voices of these children highlight the importance of inclusivity and understanding in our classrooms. The book beautifully captures the resilience and creativity of children. It's a must-read for educators who want to gain a deeper understanding of their students' diverse experiences."
James Grocott, deputy headteacher, Suffolk, UK
@deputygrocott

"This book was for me personally one of the best books I've ever read, and trust me, I'm really picky about my books! It showed me that being different isn't something that you need to change!"
Ayla, 10, Washington DC, USA

✶ ✶

DIFFERENT LIKE US!

inspiring real-life stories from kids everywhere

Margaret Rooke

Illustrated by Tim Stringer

Jessica Kingsley Publishers
London and Philadelphia

First published in Great Britain by Jessica Kingsley Publishers
An imprint of John Murray Press

1

Copyright © Margaret Rooke 2025
Illustrations Copyright © Tim Stringer 2025

The right of Margaret Rooke to be identified as the Author of the Work has been asserted by her in accordance with the Copyright, Designs and Patents Act 1988.

All rights reserved. No part of this publication may be reproduced, stored in a retrieval system, or transmitted, in any form or by any means without the prior written permission of the publisher, nor be otherwise circulated in any form of binding or cover other than that in which it is published and without a similar condition being imposed on the subsequent purchaser.

The information contained in this book is not intended to replace the services of trained medical professionals or to be a substitute for medical advice. You are advised to consult a doctor on any matters relating to your health, and in particular on any matters that may require diagnosis or medical attention.

Content Warning: Please be aware this book contains depictions of loss of a loved one, discussions of mental health, anxiety and grief.

The fonts, layout and overall design of this book have been prepared according to dyslexia friendly principles. At JKP we aim to make our books' content accessible to as many readers as possible.

A CIP catalogue record for this title is available from the British Library and the Library of Congress

ISBN 978 1 80501 292 4
eISBN 978 1 80501 294 8

Printed and bound in Great Britain by Bell & Bain Limited

Jessica Kingsley Publishers' policy is to use papers that are natural, renewable and recyclable products and made from wood grown in sustainable forests. The logging and manufacturing processes are expected to conform to the environmental regulations of the country of origin.

Jessica Kingsley Publishers
Carmelite House
50 Victoria Embankment
London EC4Y 0DZ

www.jkp.com

John Murray Press
Part of Hodder & Stoughton Ltd
An Hachette Company

The authorised representative in the EEA is Hachette Ireland,
8 Castlecourt Centre, Dublin 15, D15 XTP3, Ireland (email: info@hbgi.ie)

To Mylene, Pip, Jim, and all those like you,
doing so much for children in schools

Contents

- Introduction 9

Ch 1: Never Giving Up 15
Cora, 10, Georgia, USA 17
Dee, 13, North East England 21
Dylan, 14, Dunbartonshire, West of Scotland 25
Maizee, 13, Gloucestershire, England 31
Makaela, 10, Oklahoma, USA 35
Connor, 12, Virginia, USA 37

Ch 2: Accepting Ourselves 43
Afua, 14, London, England 44
Frida, 13, Utrecht, Netherlands 49
Oliver, 15, Yorkshire, England 53
Olivia and Alisa, both 9, London, England 57
Finn, 13, London, England 64
Emma, 13, Oklahoma, USA 69

Ch 3: What I've Learnt — 73

Isha, 13, Kolkata, West Bengal, India	75
Quinn, 12, California, USA	81
Dylan, 14, London, England	85
Mykhailo, 8, Ukraine and Liverpool, England	91
Lucas, 8, Kent, England	93
Spencer, 13, Texas, USA	97

Ch 4: Making Change Happen — 103

Jensen, 10, Belfast, Northern Ireland	105
Sarah, 14, County Galway, Ireland	109
Saphia, 15, London, England	115
Kais, 9, Merseyside, England	121
Luna, 13, London, England	125

Ch 5: Receiving Help — 129

Josie, 10, Bath, England	131
Robyn, 10, Lancashire, England	135
Lorcan, 10, London, England	141
Abubakarr, 14, Eastern Region, Sierra Leone	145
Hugh, 10, Victoria, Australia	149
Viktoriia, 8, Ukraine and Merseyside, England	155
Mia, 7, Oklahoma, USA	157

Ch 6: Making Me Stronger — 159

Aidan, 13, Cumbria, England	161
George, 11, Greater Manchester, England	165
Tamala, 14, Central Region, Malawi	171
Gracie, 13, Somerset, England	173
Sienna, 10, Kent, England	179

Ch 7: Finding the Positives ——————— 183

Riya, 11, London, England   184
Thiago, 10, Merseyside, England   189
T, 13, London, England   193
Caitlyn, 12, Oklahoma, USA   199
Isaac, 12, Norwich, England   201
April, 8, Newcastle, England   203
Hugo, 12, Buckinghamshire, England   207

- Well, What Did You Think?   210
- Some Questions for You to Answer   212
- Advice from Someone a Bit Older Than You   214
- A Chat with One Parent   217
- A Few Ways Schools Can Help   220
- Just Some of the Many Places Where You Can Go for Support   227
- Books You May Like   235
- Acknowledgements   236
- With Thanks to...   237

Introduction

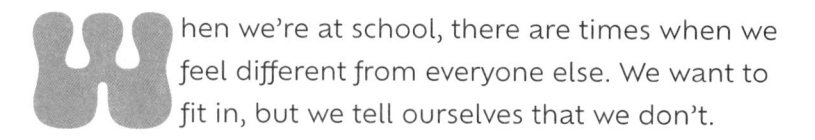

When we're at school, there are times when we feel different from everyone else. We want to fit in, but we tell ourselves that we don't.

If we're starting somewhere new, we may look at classmates who already have friends and wish we were like them. We might notice others that play together easily, when for us mixing with the rest of the class is much harder.

Or we might struggle with reading or PE or another subject, and feel embarrassed about not doing well. We may have an illness or a disability. We may have a difficult situation at home that fills our minds, stopping us feeling close to our friends and concentrating on our lessons. We may come from a distant country or another culture and believe that nothing about us fits in with our new environment.

- I'm from another country
- I can't hear well
- I can't keep my mind on what the teacher's saying
- I don't fit in with the other boys
- My mum is in prison
- I don't fit in with the other girls
- I can't read very well
- My dad has died
- My tummy rumbles because I'm hungry
- I am a carer for my brother
- I don't have any friends
- I'm worried we'll lose our home
- My mum's not well
- I have a disability
- There's something wrong with me
- I can't speak much English
- I look different from the others

For all these reasons and more, we can see ourselves as separate from everyone around us. The truth is that others feel like this too. We need to hear their stories to understand that we're not alone – there are so many feelings we all have in common. That's why I've written this book.

We can all feel different in so many ways

In these pages you'll find the stories of more than 40 children and young teenagers. They've told me what makes them feel different from their classmates and how they cope with this, at school and in the rest of their lives.

They talk about when they find feeling different tough, and when it makes them feel good about themselves.

So often we want to hide our deepest feelings away. It can seem too risky to tell anyone else what we're going through, but nearly everyone in the book says it's helped them to talk to people they trust.

They find ways to use their inner strength to move forwards with their lives, never forgetting how much they have in common with others, even when they feel separate.

It's so easy to worry about looking and seeming different from all those around us. As I've said, this can be for so many reasons, from something medical or finding learning at school harder, to an issue that affects your whole family, like not having enough money or struggling to keep the home you're in.

Afua, who's 13, advises us not to be too concerned. She says:

> **"** Never forget that all those around you are much more like you than you think. We're all really the same people. We're all normal. We just have different differences."

And in the words of Luna, who's also 13:

> **"** Everyone has something different about them, but some people feel more different than others."

While we all feel as if we're not fitting in at some stage of our lives, as we get older, we learn how to deal with these feelings.

When we're younger, this isn't quite so easy. When I was four, I remember going to school for the first time and not understanding how all the other children knew how to play together. I felt like an outsider. If you talk to adults you know, they may have similar memories of feeling out of place in the class or in the playground.

At the time I felt terrible about this. I felt ashamed. I've learnt since then that feeling different and being different can bring great strengths. It can teach us so much. The young people in this book agree with this too.

People that help us

One thing I've learnt from writing this book is how many fantastic organizations exist to support children and teenagers, and how much valuable information and help is available – face-to-face, online, in books, and via telephone helplines. Some ideas about where to go for help are listed at the back of the book.

Supporting each other

Schools have some great ways to involve all their students, making sure no one feels left out. Prescot Primary in Merseyside, in the north-west of England, describes the way it encourages students to step in and support others. The school has called this "Educating the Heart". When you read the stories in this book, you'll see how many ways there are for anyone needing advice or understanding to reach out to others.

The strength we all have inside ourselves

In this book you'll find children and young teenagers who feel different for many different reasons. Just in the first few chapters you'll read the words of Saphia who has Tourette's Syndrome, which means she can't control some of the things she says and does; Oliver who has a stammer and sometimes struggles to speak clearly; Dee who is a refugee; Dylan who has a heart problem; Connor who has ADHD; and Makaela who has life-threatening allergies.

The titles of the chapters show some of the important qualities of everyone who's spoken to me, from Never Giving Up, to Making Change Happen, Accepting Ourselves, and Finding the Positives.

In fact everyone I've talked to has reached inside and found ways to make themselves feel stronger. They've spotted the good things that come with being different, many of these surprising and life-changing.

Just dip in and take a look...

CHAPTER ONE
NEVER GIVING UP

DIFFERENT LIKE US!

CORA, 10, GEORGIA, USA

PE at school causes me so much pain that most of the time I take part in my wheelchair. I have a rare condition that causes blisters and painful bumps on my feet and makes my nails grow thick and hard.* It also makes my tongue look white.

My condition is called PC for short. PC means I can't run laps because it hurts too much, and I can't jump rope. The pain feels like pressing down on a blister as hard as you can. I get infections in my nailbed, under my fingernails. This hurts like someone pounding my nails over and over with a giant hammer.

When this happens, I go to the hospital Emergency Room where they take the nails off. The whole nails. They numb my fingers first, so it doesn't hurt at the time, but afterwards it hurts so bad. I have to stop bandages or band aids, or clothing, or my sheets at night, sticking to the raw spots. It's scary and painful.

If there's any trauma to my nails, like if I knock them while I'm washing my hands, or roughhousing in the swimming pool with my friends, that's when they grow back with the infection again.

Mostly people at school are kind about my condition.

---

* Cora's condition is called Pachyonychia Congenita.

Sometimes they are mean about it and then I have to stop myself hiding in the corner to scream. I feel stressed and sad, but my friends are great. They always have my back. I only feel the same as the others at school when I'm hanging out with my friends.

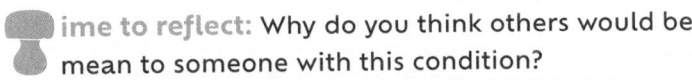**ime to reflect:** Why do you think others would be mean to someone with this condition?

One other child at school has a disability, but I'm the only one with a wheelchair. My old wheelchair was hard to push, even to go a short distance. The great news is I have a new wheelchair with a lighter frame, which is easier to use – and it's pink! It has LED lights and the front wheels glow or light up when they spin.

> "I use my wheelchair most days. I was in my wheelchair when we went to New Orleans for the Mardi Gras. As we watched the parade, people kept giving me necklaces and big giant flowers and even a teddy bear. It was like I was Mardi Gras Queen!"

Mom says I'm super smart. At school I like science, and I might work in science one day to help look for a cure for my condition. I want to raise awareness and help others who have the same as me.

I'm the only one in my family that has PC. My nails were

a little different when I was born but no doctors could figure out what was wrong. Then I was staying at a children's hospital when a skin expert asked to see photos of my nails. He had read an article and said, "It looks like PC."

Knowing what was wrong really helped. We went to a support meeting last March and I made some friends who have the same thing. One lives in Puerto Rico, and we talk on Zoom. That's special for me because we understand each other.

Question: If you had PC, would you like to speak with others with the same condition? Why is that?

I'm on pain medication and, every three or four weeks, I have the skin build up removed from my feet by a doctor, which hurts so bad. When I'm older, I'll be able to do this myself.

I have specially made pieces of metal in my shoes which help prevent the blisters and bumps that hurt me. This means I'm not able to wear sandals or flip flops or dress shoes. I'm in a big theatre show soon, and I'll be the only one not wearing special shoes. That makes me sad.

My mom has given me so much support. We have fun together too. We've started painting my fingernails. We did firework patterns at New Year, and hearts on Valentine's Day. We use stickers, paints and gel.

Everybody compliments me on my nails now. My teacher said, "Your mom's getting good!"

The teachers at my school help me if I'm unhappy. I know some teachers don't do that, but they should all be like the teachers in my school and put in more emotional support.

I give other people support too. My friend was sad the other day because she couldn't get her work done, and I said to her, "You don't have to finish it today. We have a whole other week."

> "I'm good at supporting myself. If I feel different, sometimes I sit by myself, sometimes I stand up for myself, sometimes I ignore people who say things. The best thing about feeling different is that it shows me how brave I am."

I never forget the support I get. As well as my mom, my cat, Solo, loves me more than anyone ever. He only loves me! He always makes me feel better.

DEE, 13, NORTH EAST ENGLAND

When I was nine, we had to leave Nigeria. I came to England with my mum and my little brother, and we are trying to get refugee status. I like it in this country, but they keep moving me around. First we were in Manchester, then we were in London, and now we're in the North East.

> "I don't know why they keep moving us, and I am always worried they're going to move us again. It's so hard. It means I don't make stable friendships."

Time to reflect: How would you feel if you might be moved around any day and you didn't know when that was going to happen? What would be the worst things about that?

> "I liked the school I was at in London, but up here my first school was racist. There weren't many other black kids at the school, and I was being called the worst names.
>
> I couldn't stop thinking about how they were treating me. Every night I'd be thinking, "I have to go to school again tomorrow." It stopped me sleeping and it affected how well I could do my studies."

It's important to me to do well at school, but I didn't feel safe there. I went to the teachers and told them what was happening, but they didn't believe me. The most senior teacher I approached just said, "Why are you listening to them?" It was like I was getting the blame for what they were doing.

We managed to get me moved to a different school, where there are more black kids. Here I can relax more and do things that a lot of other girls like: netball, dodgeball, acting, singing and writing my own songs.

At this school we are a big group of black people together, a lot of us from Nigeria. There are also people here who are Italian or Spanish. That's much better for me, but the worst thing is I don't know how long I'll be anywhere. I'm worried I'll get close to my friends and then be moved away again.

We've heard that we've been refused refugee status, so we're waiting for the letter to see what happens to us next. I'm worried and scared. We don't know what they'll say. I'm frightened they'll take us back to Nigeria and we can't go back there because bad things happened.

Where I am now, I like my friends. We're there for each other. One of them studies together with me. The difference between me and them is that they all come from stable homes. I feel I'm going to get moved again at any time and they don't understand. I can't tell them that. Everyone just sees me as this happy girl; nothing wrong with me. It's too much to tell people the truth. They don't know what's going on in my head. That's why I feel so different. I don't want them thinking, "Oh, she's an asylum seeker," and I don't want them to feel sorry for me. I just want life to be simpler. I want to fit in.

My friends say, "You're unique if you're different." Good friends say this from their hearts. They never talk about people behind their backs. We are all doing our best.

> "Being different has shown me I have a real strength about me. I walked away from my old school because of the racism there. I knew I could stand up for myself to the teachers.
>
> Everyone who is different should just think of themselves as being different in a good way. Everyone is different, and if you are, you're special. You have something no one else has. Look on it as a superpower. Sometimes I try to do that."

My mum has helped me so much. She is always there to make me believe in myself. She encourages me and tells me what's special about me. Parents should be there with their kids. If something's worrying them they might not want to tell you about it, but it might be really affecting them. Stay with them and stay strong. My faith has helped me too. I feel like God knows what's going to happen, he's waiting for the right time to make things better.

Schools must do more. They must listen to children who feel different and be there for them. If anything happens, they should listen to both sides of the story before they start judging. Most of the time that something bad happens, they judge the person who feels different.

Question: If you were running a school, what would you do to help children who feel scared or separate from the others?

If parents see a child is doing something wrong or not doing well, they should alert the teacher who should try to find out what is going on with the child. The kid might be trying to distract themselves from what's happening at home or avoiding everything that's worrying them.

> "I've decided to stand as a school councillor. I want to stand up for people who feel different. When people judge other people, they're not thinking about who they are, as people with feelings. Someone who is struggling might not want to talk to teachers about things. If anything bad happens to them, they need other people their age to back them up.
>
> I want to be that voice."

DYLAN, 14, DUNBARTONSHIRE, WEST OF SCOTLAND

I was born with a condition* which means my heart has four defects. I had my first procedure at four days old, my first surgery at six months, and my second surgery at 15 months.

When I was seven, I had a pacemaker fitted in my heart, but straight afterwards my lung collapsed, and I was in the worst pain. The year after I had another major operation.

Now my lungs are fine, and I can do most things. I like my school and the teachers are good. I love PE but I can't do contact sports because of my pacemaker, so I can't play rugby. School has adapted the PE programme to include me, so if we're having a rugby lesson, I've learnt the rules and can referee and do the scorekeeping. This means I'm involved in a different way.

I don't want to use my wheelchair all the time, so if I'm with my pals, I push myself to walk. I can walk the whole distance with them, but I do it in shorter sections. If I have to run, I take a rest when I need it. I've known my friends since nursery, so they understand this.

---

* Dylan's heart condition is called Tetralogy of Fallot.

DIFFERENT LIKE US!

> **Time to reflect:** Can you think of some reasons you would like friends like Dylan's?

I can't play a full 90 minutes of a football game, but I can play football. Everyone has to try to keep the ball at ground level, so it doesn't cause me any damage. I can't play baseball because you don't have any control over where the ball will go.

One thing that annoys me is that I'm not allowed to join in on laser tag games because of my pacemaker, as the lasers interfere with how the technology works.

> **"I don't spend my time feeling frustrated that I can't do everything my friends can. I'm used to it now. In fact a lot of the time I feel the same as them. Sometimes I feel different, but I try to accept this. When I was younger there was far more that I couldn't do.**
>
> **My heart condition pushes me to be better at what I can do. I never think, "I can't do that," or "That's too much for me." I am more likely to push myself and challenge myself to achieve my very best."**

I want to do PE as an extra subject at school for my exams, and the school is adapting the course so that I can do this. Hopefully this will mean others with medical issues can follow me in the future if they want to do this subject too.

DIFFERENT LIKE US!

The person who's helped me accept my heart condition most is my mum. The other thing that helps is playing on the PlayStation or the Xbox. If I thought I might have to have another operation, this would take my mind off anything that's worrying me.

At primary school* I was a bit behind because I was starved of oxygen when I was born so I have what's called a "processing delay". I struggle to get stuff down from my brain onto the paper when I'm writing. At primary I could have told you a thousand things about Formula One, but I could only have written two of these down. Looking back I am not sure I got as much support with my learning as I could have, but the teachers did help me in other ways, which was important. High school** has helped me with my learning, and I'm really pleased I've now caught up with my year.

Other people's parents should support them in the way mine have. Make sure your kids are OK. Make sure you know what is important to them and help them with these things. Parents need to be patient and friends need to be patient too because everyone is different.

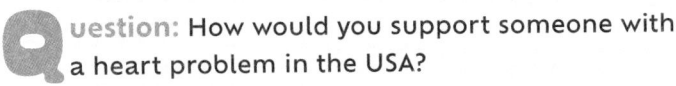uestion: **How would you support someone with a heart problem in the USA?**

---

* Elementary school
** Middle school

28

One other thing that's helped me is that I'm in the teen group of the Scottish Association for Children with Heart Disorders. We all go to the charity's family weekend events, and I go out with the teen group for days out or to eat or to the cinema. This shows me I'm not the only one with a heart condition. A whole group of us are linked in a WhatsApp group, so none of us are isolated. If one of us is in hospital, we can be in contact with others who understand.

> **"**All of this shows me that none of us is any different from anyone else. I only feel different for small amounts of time. In those moments, talking to someone about how I'm feeling is what helps."

I know at some stage in my life I might need another operation and a new pacemaker, but it's not something I spend my time thinking about. I only think about today. My first four years were difficult but recently my life has been easier. I still get breathless, but that's normal for me, and I was the only member of my family not to get Covid!

On the whole I know I'm very lucky.

DIFFERENT LIKE US!

MAIZEE, 13, GLOUCESTERSHIRE, ENGLAND

> "No matter what differences we have, we should just go for everything we want to do in life. We mustn't let anything hold us back."

I have had some difficult times, but there's so much I love doing. I go to an aerial hoop class, which means I perform above the ground like gymnasts do in a circus. I do modelling, and pageants, which are all about people being positive about their bodies. They include everyone who wants to take part. All the time I make new friends and my confidence grows.

I have epilepsy and I was bullied for the first two years of high school.* Some of the others would try to bring on seizures by flicking lights on and off. Luckily it didn't work.

In those days, people were scared to hang out with me. I stopped going out and stayed at home more. It was a bad time that only improved when a support group intervened.

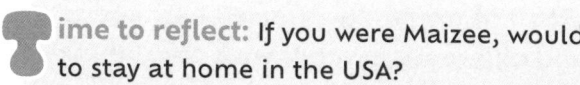

Time to reflect: If you were Maizee, would you want to stay at home in the USA?

---

* Middle school

Now I'm older and so are my friends and we can laugh when we think about the kids who behaved like that. Some of them have left the school. Now sometimes I feel different from the others and sometimes I don't. I just get on with life.

When I have seizures at school, my friends help make sure I'm OK. The school nurse is very kind and I feel close to her.

The type of epilepsy I have means I often just stare into space during a fit. I can be standing in the middle of the room not aware of anything around me. This means I miss what the teachers are saying. Sometimes I've been told I'm not listening but there's nothing I can do.

When I was younger my body used to shake. Now I get hand tremors, and these make some things difficult, especially the sewing class when I'm trying to work with a tiny needle.

> "I think I am a better person because of what I've been through. At school they always put new people next to me and my group. They say, "Maizee, I know you'll look after this person well." I think that might be because I understand disability. Most of my family is mixed heritage so I understand difference in other ways too. I think I have a good understanding of people."

The best thing for me about feeling different at school is that I don't feel I have to fit in. If you want to change who you are, that can make life hard. There's so much pressure to be the same as everyone else.

> **Time to reflect:** Why do you think Maizee might be good at looking after other people?

What's helped me most is joining clubs outside of school. It gives you friends and things you love to do in the rest of your life. Schools should get help by ringing expert organizations, like Epilepsy Action, and getting information and advice from them. They need teams of support workers to help students with differences because teachers can't do everything.

Parents should try not to overstress because that makes it harder for their kids. If they ask you "Are you OK?" and then they say "Are you *really* OK?", it's a bit over the top. It's better to keep calm and realize how strong your child is. Try to chill a bit, like your child's friends. Being different is good. We can still take on new challenges and live our lives to the best.

Note: If you are being bullied or know someone who is and want to help them, call Childline in the UK on 0800 1111. In the USA call the Stop Bullying Now Hotline on 1-800-273-8255.

DIFFERENT LIKE US!

MAKAELA, 10, OKLAHOMA, USA

I have life-threatening allergies to most foods, and being in a regular school wouldn't be safe for me, even though I have an EpiPen for when I have a reaction.

The worst thing for me is that I feel different when we eat at a restaurant. I don't get to eat what the rest of the family eats and have to bring food with me. There are some things my sister can't eat like regular ice cream and chocolate, so I'm not completely alone.

If I get an allergic reaction my skin breaks out, cracks, and bleeds. I have to put medicine on it that I hate.

> **Time to reflect:** How would you feel if you had very bad allergies?

I know other kids can eat what they want, and that makes me feel I'm not fitting in. I can't play with Play Dough because it's made out of wheat. I have to wear gloves if we're baking Christmas cookies with grandma. If someone accidentally touches me with one of the gloves, they freak out and start wiping me quickly.

> "That's actually the positive about having allergies – I can tell people really care about me because of how much they do to help."

When my sister is cooking, she is always careful to choose recipes that I can eat as well. She makes the mac and cheese that I can eat, and the ice cream sandwiches that I can eat, so I feel like everyone else. My grandma does that too when she cooks for us. She takes time to read all the details on the ingredients she uses and puts labels on the food that I can have. That's a lot of extra work for her. My mom helps by doing all this research online to find stuff that I won't react to. We don't ever give up.

CONNOR, 12, VIRGINIA, USA

In my last school I always felt out of place. I have severe ADHD which means I struggle to focus and concentrate and remember things, and I have severe dyslexia which means reading is my worst thing.

Because of ADHD, I have a hard time getting to sleep. I keep kicking my feet around. I can stop, but I always want to carry on doing it more. Some people think I'm disruptive in class and fidget too much, but I find it hard to sit still and I often need to take breaks.

I feel like my old school should maybe have been more understanding. Trying to get me to read was like asking a colour-blind person to look at colours which they can't see. It's impossible! It's like asking a sloth to run like a cheetah.

My least favourite thing is when people say things like I just need to work harder. Or I'm not trying hard enough. As if I am just lazy. It's embarrassing when they say that in front of everyone, if they are wondering why I can't read something like a menu or book. They say stuff like, "Connor, just read it. What's wrong with you?" They said I was making an excuse, but it wasn't an excuse. It's like telling a person in a wheelchair to walk. It's not that simple. Then I would get bad headaches and sometimes panic attacks. I call them ADHD attacks. This is when I started shaking and didn't know what to do. I just

DIFFERENT LIKE US!

38

broke down and couldn't read anything or even think straight. Then one time a grown up told a whole group of children that I have dyslexia, and when they said that I just wanted to burst out of there.

I did like some of my teachers, and they helped me when I was in school.

My friend Jackson helped me as well. The teachers would say, "Jackson, you can't always read for Connor," and he said to them, "Yes, I can." I was always asking for people to read the menu for me at dinner. If it's not hard for you, you won't notice how much reading there is to do in your daily life. Imagine not reading for a whole entire day, a whole lifetime. It would be pretty bad.

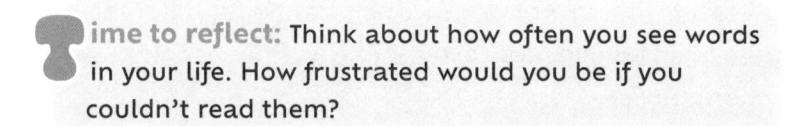

Time to reflect: Think about how often you see words in your life. How frustrated would you be if you couldn't read them?

"At the school I'm at now, a lot of people are like me, so we get each other. Honestly if I were to choose to have dyslexia or not have dyslexia, now I would say to have dyslexia. It makes me unique. It's what I am. My teacher tells me there's more benefits to having it than not having it and that's good to hear."

One thing that's hard is that my parents separated. At the time, people kept saying, "It's not your fault, it's not your problem," as if it was nothing to do with me, which I felt was straight up lying. At home I had to keep my feelings inside, because I couldn't get mad with my parents when they were arguing.

> "My parents not getting along at home meant it was hard for me at school. The teachers didn't know what I was feeling inside. It was overwhelming. So much was going on inside my head and then they expected me to sit there and do my work."

I still find it's hard for me to learn. It seems to me that other people can do things more easily. I still feel different. There's nothing wrong with being different, but I still feel like I am, even though I fit in at this school more.

> "There are some good things about feeling different. You get a better bond with someone else who's going through what you are. There are advantages that you get with dyslexia. Your brain works differently, in a good way. I heard that 13 of the presidents of the United States have been dyslexic."

Like lots of people with dyslexia, I like art. I'm not a true artist, but I'm OK. Me and my friend Corey once put this book together, "A Whale in the Sky", about being out of your element. Just try being a whale in the sky and not in the water. It was like the whale trying to be a bird, but not having wings. It can never be like a bird. That's how I felt. But it would be cool, as well, to be different from all the other whales.

Going to my new school has helped me. There's more one-on-one help and that's good for me. My teacher, Nancy, helps me here. At my last school, one of the teachers, Miss Patton, helped me. My mom and dad help me. I think all parents need to be helpful: honestly, just help your kids out; care for them; get them to a good place to make sure they can have a happy life.

I have come up with a way for all schools to help children with differences. They should all make a classroom that's only one-on-one. That means anyone who needs it can go in there. Anyone who can learn better with a teacher like that and anyone who needs time away from the rest of the class.

Question: Do you think Connor's idea is a good one for schools? Why is that?

The best friends I have had are ones who show sympathy if you're feeling bad, but not in a way that shows that you're different. I know I'm different. I know I have a hard time reading and writing.

For all of us who feel different, we must learn to ignore anyone who brings us down. The important word to remember here is the word "ignore". And tell the teacher if anyone's being mean – unless it is the teacher being mean. If it's the teacher, tell your friends or your mom.

> **"** We must keep trying, keep pushing, do the same thing we're doing. We must make sure we're around people we want to be around, to have a good environment around us, to build the best lives we can. That's what we can do – that and never give up!"

Key Question: What helps you when life gets tough?

CHAPTER TWO
ACCEPTING OURSELVES

DIFFERENT LIKE US!

AFUA, 14, LONDON, ENGLAND

Sickle cell is a condition that affects my blood cells. This was something I was born with, so there's nothing I can do about it.

When I was at primary school,* I used to get really upset, feeling different from everyone else.

The school was strict with me when it was cold weather, telling me I wasn't allowed to go outside at playtimes. I told them I didn't feel cold, but they still wouldn't let me go out. This left me by myself in the classroom while my friends were all out playing. It was so unfair.

Time to reflect: How would you feel if you weren't allowed to play outside with everyone else?

The other thing I didn't like at that school was that they had a board up outside the staffroom which listed everyone's medical conditions and the medicine they needed to take. It was a bit annoying having my name up there, but there was nothing I could do. I know it was for my safety, and all schools have to do this, but I don't think the list should have been public like that.

Sickle cell mattered more to me at that school. At my

---

* Elementary school in the USA

ACCEPTING OURSELVES

school where I am now, the teachers actually listen to you. Here some of my best friends know about me having sickle cell. They are good listeners too. They are also funny – they're just good people.

> **❝** Sometimes I still feel different from the others at school – by that I mean I feel different on the inside, but not on the outside. I can get cramps in my legs, which is one of the symptoms of sickle cell. I'm always thirsty, so I drink loads of water and then I have to go to the toilet. In year seven* the teachers remembered I had to go to the toilet whenever I asked, but now they've forgotten. They say, 'Oh no, wait five minutes,' but if you can't wait five minutes, it's not your fault."

I remember once when we had a supply teacher. I asked to go to the toilet, and she said, "No." She was like, "You can only go if you have a medical condition." I said, "I do have a medical condition," and she said, "I don't care. I don't believe you." I never saw her at the school after that, but this didn't help me at the time. All teachers including supply teachers should know if there's any reason for students to ask to leave the room. I don't mean that our confidence should be broken, but they should be told, "If so and so needs to use the loo, you have to say yes."

∗ Sixth grade in the USA

Question: Why might it be important to tell teachers how children need to be looked after?

I sometimes worry about the future. When I'm older I don't want my children to have sickle cell. It's an underlying anxiety that the others in the class probably don't have and it sometimes plays away at my mind. I guess this makes me more cautious as a person, though I can't change anything.

Most of the time I'm fine. I think we're all the same people. We're all normal. We just have different differences. There is always something cool about being different. If everyone else has brown hair, and you're the only person who has ginger, it does make you feel special.

> "I think having sickle cell has probably helped me be a helpful and kind person, someone with good people skills. It may have made me think more deeply about other people, so that's a great thing."

Whenever I was upset in the past, my mum would be there to comfort me and make me feel better. She has always been good at making me feel the same as the others. I don't worry in the same way anymore, but in the past, I really cared about having sickle cell and she always listened.

Now, if I'm feeling down, I try not to let sickle cell be the reason I'm upset. It's part of me. It's part of who I am. I have to live with it, but I don't let it take over my whole life. I keep things in perspective.

It's so important to be positive. If you have a difference, whether it's affecting your appearance, or if it's to do with something inside you, don't let that determine what you're going to do in life. I want to be an architect when I'm older, and I believe we should all build for ourselves the best life we can.

DIFFERENT LIKE US!

FRIDA, 13, UTRECHT, NETHERLANDS

When I was about 11 and still at primary school,* I didn't feel happy in my own skin, so I started finding ways to be happier. I didn't feel comfortable wearing what felt like girls' clothing. I didn't want long hair, or to wear dresses and skirts and stuff like that. I decided to have my own style. This wasn't always great – at the beginning I shaved all my hair off – but it helped me feel better when I bought different clothes and looked how I wanted to look.

Another thing that helped was that everyone in my class as well as the teachers thought what I was doing was quite cool. It felt like the right thing for me.

It was a confusing time of thinking I wouldn't be accepted by the girls but also knowing I would have been if I'd tried. I mostly hung out with the boys.

> **“**It was my parents who helped me most with feeling different and feeling OK with that, together with the support of my two best friends Julian and Mina. I play football with Mina and I'm in a band with Julian. They have never treated me any differently. I said to them, 'I don't feel completely like a girl,' and they said, 'That's great for you, and it doesn't change how we see you.'”

---

* Elementary school in the USA

Now I'm in high school* and it's a very accepting place where we treat each other equally. It has a Gender Sexuality Alliance group that meets on Wednesdays in breaktime. It's a bunch of kids to be with who are interested in any aspect of gender or sexuality issues and it's a good place to go. Every school should have a group like this. It brings people together, it's somewhere to have conversations and go to workshops. If it's a campaigning day, a lot of the teachers join in too.

Question: Why is it helpful to have a lunchtime group to go to where people have the same interests as you?

Now if someone does make a comment about how I look, it doesn't really affect me. I know my friends and people who know me think I'm all right. In the past some people have said things. If I'm out in public and I go to the girls' bathroom, people sometimes say, "Why are you in the wrong bathroom?" Stuff like that. It used to affect me a bit. Now I just laugh about it. Or they might say, "Why are you in a girls' football team?" It happens at times when people know they're only going to see you once so they think they can say what they want.

Sometimes these are genuine questions, like when

---

* Middle and high school age in the USA

people ask, "Do you prefer to be called a boy?" Usually, it's meaner than that.

I've found a place within myself where I feel contented. I do sometimes think, "What would it be like if I had been born the opposite gender?" – stuff like that – but I no longer think about it in a negative way.

In the past I felt different from the others at school, but now I don't feel that different at all. If we were all completely the same, life would be quite boring, and I've decided that being different in any way gives you different talents. The feelings I've lived through help me when I'm writing music and lyrics. Last week at school we had to do a dance to a piece of music and the group I was working with couldn't find the right song, so I wrote the music for us.

Time to reflect: What do you think life would be like if we were all the same?

The way I see it, writing a song is a bit like writing in a diary. You find the words you're feeling or words that you're not feeling. You make them rhyme, or you find some other way of making them feel right. When I compose on the piano, I can write music without lyrics to portray a lot of different types of energy and emotion.

It's so important to be able to go to someone you trust and talk to them, or to get professional help from a therapist. Plus for me, having an outlet like playing music, allowing me to put into words what I was feeling, helped me understand myself. Keeping a diary or voice notes could work in the same way.

> "I went through a dark period in my life. I was not happy, and getting over that with the help of my parents was quite a triumph for me. This has left me good at listening to someone who has a problem, and giving advice.
>
> I've realized it's a strength to come to terms with yourself in the way I have and to be completely OK with yourself."

It's important just to be yourself. Surround yourself with things that make you feel good and people who accept you. Having friends who treat you in the same way as they did before, just be there for you if you need them – I think that's important, unless you want them to treat you differently. If you're not feeling happy, surround yourself with things that make you feel good. Something my parents taught me that helped is that if you're feeling down it's part of life. Life has ups and downs. If you're down, you will go up again sometime. Just do your best to help this on its way.

OLIVER, 15, YORKSHIRE, ENGLAND

Most of us can't change whatever it is that makes us different. I have a stammer and trying to change it completely would be like trying to change who I am, and I don't want to do that.

Having said that, I've had a lot of help. I had a speech therapist for two years, when I was between four and six, and I can go back to her if ever I need to. She has been great. Without her I probably would have been a lot worse off and have a lot less confidence when I speak. I've been taught a lot of techniques that have helped. This means sometimes I stammer more, sometimes less.

> "I first had a stammer when I was four, and my parents had very little knowledge about what to do. Now my mum works in speech therapy for the NHS, so my stammer has changed her life too.
>
> It's important that parents don't worry too much about their children. When it comes to stammering, there are a lot of worries about the future, like will a child be bullied forever? I think the truth is that most of the time children are very accepting of one another. The future won't be as bad as you think. There are resources out there to help, so you won't be on your own."

DIFFERENT LIKE US!

I think the attitude of my schools has been to provide what I need so I can still get my education and not struggle. Maybe that's because with a stammer it's all about taking time when it's needed and not pushing me to answer questions and talk. Children who have other differences may need more specialist attention. There are things I don't like doing – public speaking is not my favourite thing – but I wouldn't have wanted to do this even if I hadn't had a stammer.

> "I find when I go running this is something that helps me. It's a way of concentrating and not thinking about anything. It means keeping my head down and cracking on."

Question: If you have something that worries you, would going for a run or going out into the fresh air help you? If not, what would make you feel better?

I only remember someone asking me about my stammer once. She wasn't being cruel or bullying, she was just interested in why I repeated words. I like it when someone asks me what they can do to help me. I think it shows that they care.

I have a great group of friends, but I don't think I've talked to them about stammering. I think they're all aware I have a stammer, but it's not a massive deal to me and I think they just accept it.

If I have to speak under pressure, I'm more conscious of stammering, like if I'm at a till at a supermarket, where there are people waiting behind me and I have to speak quickly. If I know it's going to be a stressful or an under-pressure situation, I'll think about what I'm going to say before I have to say it. This means I have one less thing to deal with when the moment comes.

Question: Is there anything you prepare in advance to help you do something well?

There are techniques you can try to use when you stammer. When you get stuck, the techniques start the flow of words again and allow them to come out. Some techniques work for some people and don't work for others. It's all about finding the ones that work for you, by chatting to a speech and language therapist.

What's important is that schools know what the child needs and then do it. I think that's easy to say, but one plan doesn't fit everyone. For me this was simple to deal with; for others with speech and language issues, the training needed is more complex.

> "I like it when people don't make a big deal about stammering. You're not going to stop the stammer, but you can help someone with a stammer. Make sure there's as little pressure as possible on them and find out what they need to help them get their words out."

OLIVIA AND ALISA, BOTH 9, LONDON, ENGLAND

"You can't blend in when you were born to stand out." That is true! We love that quote from the book *Wonder*.*

We are two friends from the same school. One of us has a port wine stain birthmark on her face and the other one has an extra finger on her right hand.

Alisa says:
I think my extra finger is really cute. It's tiny but it's strong. Even though it's small, I can paint the nail and draw a little face on it. The finger is also useful, and I use it in lots of ways. I can hold stuff with it, even a pencil. Sometimes I hide the extra finger because I'm scared that people won't accept me because I'm different. Someone did once tell me they thought it was gross, but he was a really rude person.

This means sometimes I show my finger off, and sometimes I'm not going to risk it, but all the time I think it's special. It shows that I'm unique.

Olivia says:
I have a big, red mark on my face. Sometimes people say things like "did you get bitten?" or "did you hurt your face?" or "did you get an allergic reaction?" or

---

* Palacio, R.J. (2013) *Wonder*. London: Corgi.

DIFFERENT LIKE US!

ALISA

"did you have that when you were born?" I know that they don't mean to be mean, but it sounds a bit mean and it's a bit annoying. I think it's better when people don't make a big deal about it.

When I was younger, people kept asking my mum about my birthmark, but now they ask me. Even people I've known for a long time – it's like they've only just noticed it. The other day I had to get a test patch for laser treatment. This meant more people were looking at me afterwards, and that was a little bit weird.

I never feel really bad about my birthmark, because I know it makes me special. I like it because it makes me *me*, and all my friends like it because they're used to me.

If you look on the internet or on Instagram, you'll see people with birthmarks like mine are really cool. Some people draw designs on them. One of them, a big Instagrammer, painted hers black and stuck on loads of gold symbols. When I have a chance, I want to do something like that.

What we both think:
That quote we love from the book *Wonder* that says, "You can't blend in when you were born to stand out," is about the main character, August, who looks different from everyone else. One of the reasons we like the book is because of the way August's friends stand up for him. When the others stop hanging out with them, his friends decide they would still rather keep hanging out with August. That's what's great about good friends.

DIFFERENT LIKE US!

OLIVIA

ACCEPTING OURSELVES

When we think about the future, sometimes we feel the first day of high school* might not be the best for us. The school will be a lot bigger and loads of people won't know us. We'll be introduced to people who haven't seen us before. Maybe they won't like us?

> "We also know that everyone has something that makes them different in their own way. When we think about the class we're in now, every person has something that makes them stand out."

Time to reflect: Think about everyone in your class. Do you agree that everyone has things that make them individual?

We know that when people say mean things, we can feel a lot stronger than them. We can push them away if we don't want to be with them.

Lots of people make us feel stronger. We meet people who are role models for us. Olivia was in hospital having a check-up, and there was this cute kid, who was about two, who had one ear that didn't look like an ear, but the little boy was adorable. She loved playing with him.

Alisa saw a man at the airport who had an extra finger that was attached in a really cool way. She was so

---
* Middle school in the USA

interested, she wanted to go over and tell him that she thought his finger looked great, but her family had to rush to get on the plane.

When we think about our lives, we know that lots of people help us. Definitely our friends and our parents. Our friends don't mind what we look like at all. They just like us.

Alisa's dad helped her because he was born with an extra toe and his sister was born with an extra finger. Her dad had to have his extra toe removed. She likes his personality and attitude and that he's a strong person.

Question: Who is a strong person in your life you can learn from?

Alisa says if she feels sad or doubts herself, her cat helps her too. She somehow knows something's wrong and comes up to her and stares at her and Alisa just gives her a hug.

Olivia sometimes thinks about why she has her birthmark. She wonders if it was a great, great, great, great relative who had one and passed it down to her. Someone who is part of history.

We both think schools can help children who feel different. We think our favourite quote should be put on the wall of every school. Schools should watch out for children who have a difference, just to make sure they're not getting bullied or anything like that.

> "Lots of us have something that makes us different. We must all remember how good that is, it doesn't matter what anyone else thinks. We can just be ourselves. We can remember that, on the inside, we're all the same."

FINN, 13, LONDON, ENGLAND

At home I live with my two mums. In school there's always loads of talk about dads, things like "My dad dropped me off at school today," or "Do you want to come home? I think my Mum and Dad are there."

These conversations make me feel slightly different, but I'm not thinking, "I wish I had a dad and a mum." It's nice to feel different sometimes, and I know lots of my friends just don't really care. To them, two mums is no big deal.

The only other time I feel different is when I say to someone, "My mum did this," and my friends say, "Which one?" I can understand that it's confusing for them.

So, the way I see things, I'm similar in some ways, different in others. I'm fine about that.

Question: Is this true of everyone – that we're similar in some ways, different in others?

I go to one of the biggest schools in London. It's very busy there, but also quite a calm place, because lots of it is very orderly. There are lots of opportunities and I have good friends there. There are lots of ways to be yourself.

> **"I think when you feel different, it's easier to accept others and their differences. If there's someone who's different from the others in any way, I know what that's like; what it would be like to be them; and I can relate."**

If someone at school suddenly had a serious medical condition or lost one of their parents and it was someone I liked, I would make a real effort to be friends with them. If it happened to one of my friends, of course I'd be really loyal to them. If it happened to someone I found a bit annoying, but I knew they were having a tough time, I'd probably be a lot more understanding than if someone was having a pretty average life and they were just an annoying person.

If I'm feeling different and struggling with it in any way, I mostly deal with this inside myself. I certainly get a lot of help from my parents and my friends. Mainly I work out for myself how to deal with situations.

I haven't personally had any homophobic comments directed at me. A few years back, there was a nasty kid going around using a rude insult that included the word "gay". That was probably the worst I'd heard. To an extent, there's nothing you can really do about it, because kids are going to talk about things they don't fully understand and use them as insults and say things they don't mean. It's something that happens in schools. This was at primary school, and I spoke to my head of year who dealt with it, and I told my parents what was happening.

I think it's a good idea to speak to a teacher or to your parents if something is troubling you. What's most important is that you feel strong inside.

I don't feel like I need a father figure. I do know who my father is, and he feels more like a close uncle or something, not a dad. Two mother figures is enough parents!

One of the most important things schools can do is to have places where students feel they can talk to someone safely. This could be through an anonymous email system or a club like an LGBTQ+ club, or one to one with a teacher. Having extra support for anyone who needs it is something my school does very well, but other schools don't necessarily do this as well.

Time to reflect: Where do you find it easier to talk to someone and feel safe?

The most important thing that parents can do for their children is to listen and ask what the kid wants the parents to do. Sometimes it can be good just to have someone to tell that someone was racist or homophobic at school. You don't necessarily want your parents to do anything about that. You just want to get it off your chest. If a parent asks "What would you like me to do about that?" then you feel you have some level of control over a not very nice situation. I think that could be very helpful.

We should all be able to talk to our friends if they are close friends. It's great if you don't have to hide the fact you're going through a tough time from them. For me that's most important.

> "If you're feeling different, and there's some element of bullying, it's important to stand up for yourself. Don't let something be said to you and keep the hurt on the inside. Just talk, then others can help you deal with it yourself. Talking to someone else is a great way to find that little bit of courage. Then it's not you against the world. It's you plus your friends or plus your parents or your teacher. You're all in it together."

DIFFERENT LIKE US!

68

EMMA, 13, OKLAHOMA, USA

Having differences changes you. You solve problems in your own special way, instead of your mind just going down the same track. Being different has taught me to look out for others, and to make friends with anyone else who is different. It can make you kinder, though I think I'm a bit meaner since I became a teenager!

Me and my brother and sisters were all fostered and then adopted into the same family. We all have medical conditions. We go to a charter school called Epic – we school at home and our teachers are on Zoom. If we need help, there's a tutor who can help us.

I have a tracheostomy – a hole in my windpipe. This allows air to reach my lungs. My trach is my lifeline. I couldn't breathe without it.

I feel frustrated about this, sometimes to the point of breaking things. It means I can't run for a long time without being given oxygen. If I went swimming with my cousins, the other kids wouldn't be allowed to splash, as the water might go onto my trach. That means they lose out on fun, so I don't go.

I have an on-going brain bleed also. It's another thing that blocks me from doing the stuff other kids do.

One thing I can't do is be around dust. Our grandpa

made our school desks from wood using special tools. He's so talented. He once made a stool in under five minutes. I would like to be around to watch him do that, but I can't.

I can't eat ice cream or chocolate as it goes into my trach. If I breathed it into my lungs, I could get pneumonia. If my brother caught that from me there's a good chance he would die, as he has almost no immune system.

Because of our medical conditions, we live almost a quarantined life. That means we can't have friends round, but it also means we do get to watch loads of telly. We watch a lot of police and medical shows and talk about them as a family because that's something we enjoy and some of us want to work in those fields when we're older. My sister Caitlyn wants to be a doctor and she got to see her first sterile procedure when our brother Joey was in hospital, and that was exciting for her.

> "When I was born, I was hearing, but since I was four, I've gradually lost my hearing. We don't know why. Despite this, I don't see a glass as half empty. If you see a glass as half full, it makes life a little easier."

Question: Are you impressed that Emma is such a strong and positive person?

ACCEPTING OURSELVES

There have been times when I felt completely accepted. Caitlyn once secretly taught all the students and the teacher in our class the alphabet in sign language without me knowing. On the last day of school, they all surprised me by singing and signing to me.

Another time was when they opened our local zoo in the evening for families with disabilities. A lot of the people there were deaf, and they had interpreters there for the zookeeper talks. I felt so included.

As a family we've had many acts of kindness. One was on a trip with the Make a Wish charity when our whole meal was paid for by another diner. Families with disabled children don't have spare money because of the equipment we have to pay for, so this helped our mom.

Time to reflect: Why does being kind help people?

Because of my hearing loss, I use books to pick up what I need that helps me stand up for myself. You can learn so much by reading. I also find friends in other parts of the country who are deaf. We Zoom with each other and give each other strength.

A kid once told the author Temple Grandin, who is autistic, "Thank you for showing me that my brain is just different, not broken." It's a powerful message that tells us we are not alone and there are others out there like us.

DIFFERENT LIKE US!

> "My own advice for anyone who feels different is to find friends who accept you and support you as you are. That's so much better than trying to change yourself.
>
> I also say don't be afraid to stand up for yourself and others. You may have something different about you, but it doesn't change everything. On the inside you're just the same, and the inside is all that matters."

Key Question: What about you makes you stand out and feel proud?

CHAPTER THREE
WHAT I'VE LEARNT

DIFFERENT LIKE US!

ISHA, 13, KOLKATA, WEST BENGAL, INDIA

When I was five, I had unbearable pains in my joints and bouts of fever. I was diagnosed with a serious disease.* I went to a national hospital for treatment, and they saved my life.

Because of the side effects of the chemotherapy, I had to stop my education. I wanted to go back to school after two years – doing well in school is very important to me – but I couldn't.

When I was finally allowed back, my teachers were very kind to me. They teach me well. I have great friends too, but not everyone is kind.

Every student at school has to wear an identity badge that says our name and how old we are. Since I missed out on my education for several years, sometimes my classmates look at my identity badge and make fun of me. I am much older than they are, and they think I'm a failure and that I've retaken my school years many times. This is not the case. They don't know I had a serious disease. I don't tell them because I don't think they would understand.

My main fear is that if I tell them about my illness, the

---

*Isha had blood cancer, but the word cancer is not commonly used in India.

teachers will come to know I've told them, and I will get into trouble. We don't talk about these things in India.

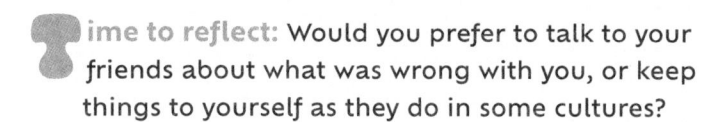

Time to reflect: Would you prefer to talk to your friends about what was wrong with you, or keep things to yourself as they do in some cultures?

Because I can't tell anyone about my illness, I feel different and embarrassed. I wish I was in Year 8 not Year 6 because then I wouldn't have to face this humiliation. The strange thing is that I don't feel different because I had the disease. I am now cured, so in that way I am the same as them, though I find studying all the time tiring, and I struggle to play sports in school because I get exhausted.

One thing that made things worse while I was being treated was that my father left. He now lives hundreds of miles away. My mother works long hours to pay the bills, and we don't have a permanent place to live. Life can be hard.

When I was ill, my grandmother who lived with us believed I was contagious, even though all the doctors said it wasn't catching. This is what happens in India. She made me eat and drink separately and I felt isolated and alone. My friends weren't allowed to play with me, as their mothers thought they might catch my disease and I was too young to understand what was going on. I started to believe I was contagious too.

I felt like crying a lot of the time, and the question "why me?" still haunts me. I still question why I was seen as "untouchable" in this way.

All of this means I have been through a lot that the others at school cannot understand. The chemotherapy was harsh. I still think about it. Why did I have to suffer so much? The pain, the sickness and the hair loss? I get angry and ask God again "Why me?" but there is no reply.

> "The other difference between me and my class is that I know what it's like to feel weak and ill, and now I feel strong. This is a good thing. I have no doubt about how strong I am, and that I have the ability to move ahead in life despite my drawbacks. I am doing well in my studies and I plan to work very hard and do even better. I also dance and draw well so I am achieving a lot. This brings me so much determination and motivation."

I had to grow up and mature quicker than most girls my age. I have to look after myself a lot as my mother is out at work, and I have a lot of responsibilities in the house. I find ways to use my intelligence to give me strength and create the picture of a bright future for us.

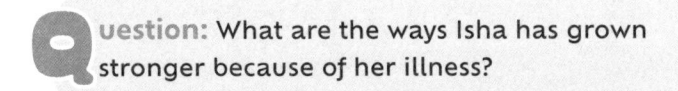

Question: What are the ways Isha has grown stronger because of her illness?

When I think about it, I wish schools would be more open with their students. I want to tell the others, "Don't say these things about me, they hurt." I wish the class teacher would scold the students that tease me and tell them they will be punished, but it isn't part of our culture to speak openly like that.

I want the others to know that just because I am the eldest in my class and just because I had a "disease", I am not different inside. I am not inferior or stupid. They should not judge me on my age. They don't know my story. No one should tease or hurt other children.

> "I also believe that if you can stand on your own two feet, then it doesn't matter if you are different. My advice to all of us is stand up for yourself. Work hard to progress and don't worry about little things that upset you. When you produce good results, no one can touch you."

I fought the disease, so I know I am powerful. I know I can progress without my father, and no matter what other people say to put me down, I will learn not to listen.

My inner strength comes from my mother who has been my constant support, together with one of my aunts. There's also a wonderful charity* that helps look after

---

* The Cancer Fight Foundation

me, with volunteers I call my "aunts". They played with me, read to me, and bought me gifts during my treatment. They helped me find dance lessons and this led to me performing in front of others, which gave me great confidence. They still pay for my education.

> "To move on I want to put my bad experience aside and concentrate on moving forwards. In the future, I want to live well. Sometimes I want to be a doctor as I know the good they can do. Sometimes I think I can be a lawyer because I believe strongly that I know right from wrong. There are so many things that I want to be.
> I will work hard and show everyone I can create the future I want."

DIFFERENT LIKE US!

QUINN, 12, CALIFORNIA, USA

My school is for kids with dyslexia, so people think my life must be easier, but it doesn't work like that.

> "It's hard to be in a reading group in a dyslexia school and feel like you're still the one who struggles with reading out loud. It's tough when we can all be reading this story and everybody else manages before me. I feel like the lowest in the group."

I think a lot of people at the school were reading naturally and just needed a little bit more help, or they've been at the school longer, so they've learnt more stuff.

This leaves me thinking I'm more dyslexic than they are. It's not easy for me to take notes during the lessons because I'm not good at typing. After school, I find the homework hard, especially reading and writing.

My school is small with not a lot of students. One thing that helps me is that they hold fun events, like musicals which are big productions, and three times a year we get to choose a class with a choice of subjects. I've done knitting and bracelet making.

The best things at school are being with my friends, and

I love PE class because we get to run around and get our energy out.

Time to reflect: What do you enjoy at your school?

Out of school I enjoy gymnastics and drawing. I love designing dresses and rooms, and I love my dogs. They are funny, especially one of them who's clumsy and he does a lot of silly things like flipping over when he's trying to reach a toy I'm holding up.

I've known one of my friends outside school since I was a little baby. She's good at reading, so if we're doing anything together, she always does the reading bit. Because I've known her my whole entire life, I can be myself with her.

> "Feeling different from the others at my school means I've become sensitive to other people who feel excluded or separate. I think I'm good at reading the room. When I graduated fifth grade,* I was awarded the Friendship Award by the school I was at. They only gave out two awards and one went to me."

I felt more different at my old school before I moved here, because every time we had to go to a writing class

---

* Year six in the UK

or had to read, I would have to go to a tutor. I even had to miss recess to go to the tutor across the street. At the time I was really annoyed. I was having a conflict with two friends – we were fighting over one friend – and this meant I missed the time of hanging out with that friend.

I called myself stupid a lot in those days, because I was comparing myself to the other kids, and my mom made me a book called Brilliantly Dyslexic, with famous dyslexic people in it to show me I wasn't stupid and that these people felt the same as me when they were young.

Question: How would you help your child if they felt they weren't clever?

Schools need to know that there will be different challenges for each person with dyslexia so you can't know one person with dyslexia and think everyone is the same. I find it so annoying when I'm compared with other people with dyslexia. Everyone has their own story. People say to me, "My son's dyslexic. I know what things are like for you." Well, you probably don't. I think they should get better training for teachers, and people should have more tutors, because tutors have helped me.

The other thing I find annoying is when people say something at school is not that hard at all. I'm struggling and they're saying, "Oh, this is easy. How can you not do this?"

I know I'm not going to feel better immediately. There's not a lot that can automatically be all fixed. It's going to take time, but this school is better than the last one. Things will get better eventually.

DYLAN, 14, LONDON, ENGLAND

When I was younger, people were constantly annoying me in the class by tapping on my back. In the breaks they barged and pushed into me. When I told them to stop, they started again, twice as much, then three times as much. Then I stormed out of the room and into the toilets. The teacher said I couldn't storm out of the room like that, and I said, "I just don't care."

They were picking on me because I am autistic. They had spotted some differences in me, and I couldn't do anything about that.

> **"The teachers told me to stop listening to what the others were doing or saying. They were saying, 'Ignore this, ignore that, do this, do that,' but I didn't want to be the one making all the changes. What about the others – why didn't they tell them to leave me alone? I can't cope the same way as other people can in bad situations."**

I always knew I was different but in primary* I wasn't old enough to understand what the difference was. I tried to blend in with the others. I tried walking around with them or asking them if they'd be friends with me but neither of these strategies worked. I felt I was the

---

* Elementary school in the USA

DIFFERENT LIKE US!

same, and I didn't understand where I wasn't the same. If someone else with autism had been with me, that would have been worse. I wouldn't have wanted to see them being treated like I was.

The moment my dad told me that I didn't have to go to that school anymore, I was jumping up and down with joy. If your child is feeling down, parents should intervene quickly, not wait for things to get even worse.

Question: What would you do if your child was unhappy at school?

At first I thought secondary school* would be better, but I don't think it was. The teachers were at the school just to teach; to me they didn't seem to care about anything else.

I'm starting a new school soon, and I'm excited to go, but I think I'm just going to go there for the education, then come straight home and live my life. I don't want to make friends, but no one understands that. I've realized I'm not one of those "friends" kind of guys. Adults try to understand me, but they don't succeed. There are so many extra aspects to me that they're just not able to cope with. Now I just want time to myself.

Adults don't understand when I want peace and quiet.

---

* Middle and high school in the USA

I say, "Don't come near me," and they won't leave me alone. It's hard living in a world where people don't understand.

I have learnt some important lessons. I've learnt that if I try at something and fail a couple of times – like trying to make friends – I shouldn't keep trying. It will just get worse. Do something else instead. Otherwise, people get annoyed at you.

I've found ways of losing myself from reality. There's a game I love playing and that helps me feel good about myself. I want to become a pro at it and that takes practice and practice and I'm willing to do that.

My mum and dad say to me that life is going to get better, and I do think it will. I just have to wait until it does. I'll wait until something good happens, no matter how long it takes. Everyone should do that. Do not give up on yourself.

I think teachers need more training to support everyone to the best of their ability. Even if they don't know much about someone, they should do their best to support them. You can't tell an autistic person to "do, do, do" and expect them to do everything you tell them to. They can't do that, and it will just get worse for everyone. They won't fully understand what you're talking about.

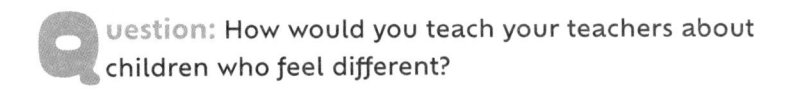

Question: How would you teach your teachers about children who feel different?

> **❝ There are so many aspects to myself that I don't know yet, but I know there are strengths in being different. I can name every single player and their squad number and where they play on a football pitch in the Premier League, both the starting elevens and bench. I'm good at drumming, drama, and streaming – creating content for people to watch. I've been doing that for many years and I'm making money with advertising and subscriptions.❞**

My advice to anyone who feels different is don't change who you are. Keep going, and if people don't like you, they don't like you. If people like you, they like you. Do whatever you can with your life to make things better, but don't change your personality. Be true to yourself and who you are, no matter what other people think.

DIFFERENT LIKE US!

MYKHAILO, 8, UKRAINE AND LIVERPOOL, ENGLAND

Because of the war, I'm over in the UK from Ukraine. I'm here with my mum, my brother, and my grandparents. My dad and cousin are still in Ukraine. I miss them a lot, and I miss my dog and my house.

> "When I'm missing my dad and my cousins and friends at home, talking about this makes me feel better, and phoning my dad always helps me. Then I know he's safe and well. It's always great to talk to him."

School here is very good, and the teachers help me. Thanks to them, I'm proud of myself for how I've settled here. It helps me that I love playing football. This means I play with my friends here just as I played with my friends in Ukraine. I think if any children feel different from the others for any reason, football is a great way for them to feel better. Once my friend Rosco was sad. The first thing I did was to ask him to play football with me. Not everyone likes football, so the other thing you can do is go up to them and ask them what game they want to play. So don't treat them differently; treat them the same as everyone else.

It's important for schools to talk to children and understand them. When I first arrived, my teacher learnt some words in my language to help me feel at home. She sat me next to Rosco, who is still my friend now.

Question: How has Mykhailo's school helped him?

At first, I couldn't speak any English at all. I had to draw and act things out to communicate. Now I know much more. Just before the Eurovision Song Contest, we painted a giant Pysanka egg which is a symbol of Ukraine. My mum came into school and gave advice about what we should put on it, like images of birds, flowers, cakes, and Ukrainian pasta. They displayed the egg in the city centre to celebrate the links between Liverpool and Ukraine.

> "My English is a lot better, and I've made lots of friends. I've taught the others in my class some Ukrainian and we've just made Ukrainian food together. So they teach me and I teach them."

LUCAS, 8, KENT, ENGLAND

> ❝One of the people who's helped me in my life is my dad, even though he's in prison. What he's done has made me realize at a young age that I want to live my life differently from the way he has. I've learnt how important it is to be kind and respectful, and that's helped me with life a lot. I think it's one reason why I haven't been in trouble at school. The teachers don't ever need to tell me off.❞

My friends are people who also follow the rules. They've never been unkind, and they don't annoy me. I know it's important to be with kind people. Some people know this, but they still don't do it.

I think because of everything that's happened to me I've become mature earlier than some of the others who are my age. I know how to stand up for myself. People tell me I'm incredibly kind and I think I really am.

My school is quite good. The only thing I think that they could do better is acknowledge that my dad's in prison more. I don't mean in front of the class; I mean one of the teachers talking to me about it, asking how I'm feeling, just now and again. When I do talk about Dad to people it's always a big conversation, like with my mum, but it helps just to have short talks as well.

DIFFERENT LIKE US!

94

On the other hand, if the teachers do talk about it to me, it makes me feel more different from the others, and sometimes I like to feel the same.

On Father's Day they used to let me make two cards at school, one for my dad and one for my stepdad. Now they don't and that makes me feel my dad is a bit forgotten.

At school, even my best friends don't know about my dad being in prison, and I've been playing with them since year two.* I think I've been forced to grow up a bit quicker than the rest of the class and I just want to keep some things to myself. I don't think the others would understand.

> **Time to reflect:** Are there things you want to keep secret and not tell anyone else?

One thing I'm good at is helping myself to become a stronger person. I like testing myself to show I can do things that scare me, things that show me how strong I am. I did this Treetops Experience for adults with my stepdad. It was high up in the trees and I was up there for two hours. That's how long it took us to finish it. I was scared I was going to fall, even though I had a harness on, but I didn't.

---

* First grade in the USA

I also have ways to comfort myself. When I feel sad, I can talk to one of my teddies, or I go to sessions at a local charity. I used to talk with a teaching assistant at school.

> "If anyone feels different and they want to talk about it, it's so important that they can. If you brush whatever is upsetting you under the carpet, it might build up your anxiety. Parents need to listen to what their children are saying and answer their questions. They need to stop doing what they're doing, like washing up, and give them their full attention. That would be ideal. They could encourage their children to find comfort in their toys, as this has helped me.
>
> It doesn't need to be a person who helps you. We can help ourselves. Sometimes just talking to ourselves or thinking to ourselves can help us understand and make us feel better."

SPENCER, 13, TEXAS, USA

There are lots of things I'm good at. I am a good runner, soccer player, and reader. I'm good at math and great with animals.

I learn differently and it can take me longer to master skills. One of the ways I learn is by copying others. When my dad was dying, I was seven years old. I worked out how his oxygen machine worked, and I could fix it when its alarm went off. I've learned how to cook and do laundry by watching people. I've realized I notice things other people don't. It's kind of one of my superpowers!

I was six months old when my mom found out my dad was sick. He was exposed to chemicals in the Air Force. This meant I could never do a lot of things with him, like going to sports events or playing ball. When we knew he was going to pass away, Mom bought him greetings cards so he could write them for me. I get one every birthday. I just turned 13 in January, and I got one then. The cards are very special to me because I don't remember him very well. I'll get one on my 18th birthday and there's one for when I graduate. My mom also kept samples of his voice for me to hear, so I can always remember what he sounded like.

I missed a lot of school when Dad died. My teachers didn't want me to repeat a year, but my mom, who is a

DIFFERENT LIKE US!

teacher also, thought it would be the best plan for me. I ended up having to go to school with kids younger than me. I'd like to be right in the middle age-wise. I think that would be easier.

When there are dads' events at school and Mom turns up instead of my dad, I have always felt embarrassed because she was the only mom there. I told her I didn't want her to come. It made my mom sad for a moment, but still she shows up. She never gives up on me, no matter how tough being different has been for me. She has made me tougher and stronger.

I was born with a genetic condition, and I also have ADHD, mild autism, and anxiety. I know I'm different. My ADHD is bad sometimes. I have a hard time staying still and concentrating in class. I'm also a TK – or teacher's kid. My mom is a teacher at the high school in my district and my stepdad, Alex, is a teacher at the middle school,* which is my school. This means they find out about whatever I've done before we get home every day.

Time to reflect: Do you think it would be tough to be a teacher's kid?

The ADHD also is a problem for me because I'm easily distracted, especially in the afternoon. The other day I was playing a game instead of doing my math test.

---

* Years eight and nine in the UK

I have to start doing better or I'll never get my Pokémon cards back that my mom has put in time out. I also do things accidentally or absent mindedly and other kids get mad. Someone bumped into me at lunch because they thought I was cutting in line, but I wasn't.
Why can't people be more accepting and patient?

> "I'm trying hard not to get myself in trouble, but my classmates aren't the most patient or kind to me at times, and I don't like being picked on. I get teased when I cry at school and I'm called a teacher's pet, because the teachers help me when they hear I'm being bullied. Then they call my mom or stepdad, but I don't want special treatment like this because it makes the other kids meaner."

I used to do this thing that people thought was weird – rubbing my hands together when I was anxious. Then I stopped doing that but started scratching my head. Now I pull the threads out of clothes, so I have socks with holes in them. I think that's better than scratching. I want to act normal because if I don't, I'm not going to get any more friends.

Key Question: What are the things you've learnt about yourself from feeling different?

> "I hope that school will get easier. As I get older, I am better able to stand up for myself. I like being alone sometimes as I can read my books and not be told how weird I am. I become confident about my own abilities. It makes me feel self-sufficient. You can't presume every kid always wants to be with other kids. I like being able to enjoy myself without having to think about what others think."

CHAPTER FOUR

MAKING CHANGE HAPPEN

DIFFERENT LIKE US!

JENSEN, 10, BELFAST, NORTHERN IRELAND

From when I was born, I couldn't hear with my left ear, and my right ear always has infections and other problems. Once, when I was in the playground with my mum, someone saw us signing to each other. This is how we talk using our hands. Some of the other parents asked us about what we were doing and how it helps me to understand.

That's when I started making wee videos for the class, teaching the others to sign to each other like me and Mum do. Sign language is really fun. Chocolate is my favourite word to sign – it looks like a messy chin and makes me think of getting chocolate everywhere.

We posted the videos on Facebook and then the deaf charity, the RNID, posted them and they went viral. So many people saw them! It's been like a rollercoaster since. I've been on the TV news and everything. Once I stood in front of my whole school and taught them how to sign.*

I like that my videos show other people how to learn the language. This means that if they come across someone who's deaf, they can communicate with them. A lot of the teachers are learning sign language now and

---

* See Jensen's YouTube channel, Jensen's Antics: www.youtube.com/@jensensantics6600

every year the whole school signs one of the Christmas carols we sing. One of my teachers even wants to be a sign language teacher. We used to have 26 languages spoken at our school. Sign language is now our 27th.

My school is big with lots of students. I have some one-on-one lessons, but for the rest I'm in the class with everyone else. Sometimes I feel different from the others as I have to sit at the very front of the class. I find that if someone is talking and I'm not looking at them I miss what they're saying. When I'm playing football, I don't hear very well. There are no deaf football teams in Northern Ireland. Maybe I should set up my own?

Besides my hearing problems, I'm like everyone else. I like playing football and I like playing with my cousins and my friends. My best friends are all understanding because of my hearing, and there's a boy in the class with autism and we look out for him as well.

> "When I feel different from the others, I feel a wee bit sad and left out. A wee bit lonely. This sometimes happens in the playground – it's hard to hear people when it's noisy. Sometimes people can be mean, just because I'm different."

Time to reflect: What would your life be like if you couldn't hear well?

I think of myself as a kind person, and I think being deaf has made me kinder. If people are struggling, I help and encourage them.

> **❝ I never give up and I like proving people wrong. If there's a challenge, I say, "Just watch me." Someone once said to me, "I bet you can't score from the halfway line", and I did – but I felt bad for the keeper."**

Sign language means I have a deaf community of friends as well as my school friends. I go to groups run by Action Deaf Youth. This helps me because at school I'm one of only two people with hearing difficulties, but at the group everyone is deaf, even the group leaders.

My mum has helped me the most. She gives me inspiration. She learnt sign language and helps me when I'm struggling with stuff. She showed me other people who made sign language videos and made me see I wasn't the only one.

I've had two failed surgeries on my left ear. One lasted four hours. After that I had to keep my head still for six weeks and that's not easy. Mum looked after me all that time.

Time to reflect: How hard would it be to keep your head completely still for six weeks, even at night?

> "If anyone has something different about them in your school, I think people should play with them and be kind. Make them feel welcome. The school should support them. Parents should always be proud of them.
>
> I want people to know it's OK to be different. Everyone is different. Just be a good friend to them. That will help them believe in themselves and be confident because they are great people. They can achieve what they want, no matter what it is."

I know that if I hadn't had a problem with my hearing, I wouldn't have achieved half of what I've done, and that's really exciting.

SARAH, 14, COUNTY GALWAY, IRELAND

When some of my friends are meeting up and going out after school, I'm at home helping to care for my sister, Esther. I wouldn't choose to live any other way.

Esther is two and she has Down Syndrome, a heart condition, and other complex medical needs. Mum and Dad work hard looking after her, doing her physiotherapy and hospital visits, as well as looking after my three younger brothers. I do my best to get my homework done at school, then when I get home at 4pm, I help too.

One of the things I do is help with Esther's speech therapy, finding ways to encourage her to talk. I love it. Sometimes I help with her medications. We have to be precise to make sure she gets exactly what she needs. At one point this had to be done through a tube that went into her stomach and it was really complicated.

We're now in the middle of a struggle to keep Esther's glasses on her face and stop her from breaking them. They've been broken four times this year. Each time we have to ship them to the UK to get them repaired. She doesn't have good eyesight and the optician says the more she wears her glasses, the better she will see in the future. She also has a low level of diabetes, and we have to be careful to give her a balanced diet.

DIFFERENT LIKE US!

Whenever there are hospital trips for Esther, I help take care of my young brothers, making breakfast or lunch, helping with homework, and putting them to bed.

Everyone loves Esther. She is so much fun. She likes doing silly faces and loves playing this game when we all try to stay serious and it doesn't last for more than five seconds, and then she starts laughing and we all just start laughing.

If I'm playing cards with my friends, she takes some cards and pretends she knows how to play. Other times, she pretends she knows how to read.

All my friends love spending time with Esther. They're very supportive of me and how much time I spend caring for her, even if this means I can't go out with them as much as I would otherwise.

Time to reflect: What would your life be like if you needed to care for a family member like Sarah does?

Every young carer feels different at school because some of the others don't understand what our lives are like. Even some teachers don't understand. In that sense life can be a little bit hard. Overall, I have to say I've had good support from my parents, my friends, and from some of my teachers.

It also helps if your parents support you well. If I'm too

busy, my parents always say, "You have loads of study, you don't need to help us today." Or if they notice I'm tired they say, "It's OK to leave it to us." I know that isn't always the case with some of the others who care for family members.

> "I think life is harder for young carers who don't want anyone to know they are young carers. They may be shy or just not want other people to know about what's happening in their family. It's tougher for them than it is for me. They don't get the support or understanding.
>
> Schools should do more to find out what problems their students might be facing that make life more difficult and raise awareness about these issues to every single student."

I am part of the Young Carers group in Family Carers Ireland. Every Wednesday we have an online group Zoom meeting. We do something together like baking or drawing.

Because of the support I have, I would say a lot of the time I feel the same as the others in my school. Obviously they don't understand the impact on me of the hospital trips and why these mean I can't go uptown with my friends, but they respect me for what I do. They would never make fun of me. If anyone doesn't like the way being a young carer gives me the opportunity to speak out in public, I would say to them there are 60,000 young carers in Ireland and only two or three of us are willing to speak up on behalf of all of them. People need to hear what life is like for us.

> **"** Everyone's unique. Somebody can be amazing at football, somebody can be amazing at hurling, and someone can be great at caring and speaking out for other carers. I wouldn't want to change things. I like things the way they are. I think my caring responsibilities expand me as a person."

When I'm older I want to be a neurosurgeon, so I take my schoolwork very seriously. In my spare time, when other people might be reading about romance or an adventure, I'll be reading about neurology.

One of my strengths is being responsible. That's one thing I had to learn quickly. I feel I'm good with people. I like talking to them and listening. If they have a problem, they know they can come to me.

Time to reflect: In what ways do you think you would be good at caring for one of your family?

There was a Young Carer of the Year ceremony last year and I was given the award for the province where I live. That was a great moment, but caring is, of itself, a reward for me. It's given me a lot. I feel it's helped me to be a better person. Before Esther was born I kind of took life for granted. Afterwards I realized how great it is when you're able to see your mum and dad when you want to, because I didn't see them for the first few weeks of her life.

I think all parents should encourage their children and be there for them. Tell them they're unique; that what they're doing can help change the world. Make sure your child knows how proud you are of them.

> "Everyone who feels different should be proud of who they are. If they have a disability or a problem in their life, they can raise awareness about this and change other people's lives. This will help them realize that what makes them different is not the end of the world. They can turn it into something positive that the world will love."

SAPHIA, 15, LONDON, ENGLAND

School is scarier and more stressful than it should be. I have Tourette's Syndrome, which means I twitch, move, and make sounds I have no control over. I can make random noises or whistle or say offensive things, or I start punching, kicking, hitting, or throwing books around. Today I was trying to listen to what my teacher was telling me to do, and I just threw my pen and books on the floor. This is so bad.

I try to suppress the tics or hold them in, but this feels painful and uncomfortable and can make them worse. If anyone asks me what the worst thing I'd ever said was, I know they don't ask me that to be rude, but it feels rude and shows how different I am from them. I've even been asked if I am faking the tics. Why would I?

One supply teacher who didn't know about my Tourette's told me off for something and my tics became worse and I swore at her. This wasn't my fault. It wasn't under my control, but she gave me a detention. The other teachers saw what happened and cancelled the detention, but I still felt bad.

My tics became much worse when I became a teenager. As well as this, I have autism, and this means I don't like a lot of noise. I've always felt that I'm being asked to fit in and am expected to fake laugh at things I don't find funny. I have seizures too. I used to have loads of

DIFFERENT LIKE US!

seizures every day. Now they're not too often and they're usually when I'm stressed or anxious. Being with my dog helps me manage these feelings, and so does music. I love Billie Eilish and Lewis Capaldi who both have Tourette's as well.

> "Being different has strengthened me. I've had to form my own opinions and keep strong values. I won't ever fit in with whatever anyone else is saying if I don't agree with them. As hard as my life is, I know that whenever I've been knocked down, I always get up and carry on. Each time I feel more powerful."

One good thing that's happened is that they've set up a room at school called The Hub for kids who need a bit of a break. I think if it wasn't for me and my needs that room might not be there. It is a quiet space with a beanbag and a table, and you can work or just sit. The school is also good at updating all my teachers about how I am, and they've given me a reduced timetable. Although phones are banned in my school, I'm allowed to use mine because music helps me so much.

Time to reflect: Why do you think a quiet place at school helps people who feel different?

I've given talks to my teachers and my class and to a local youth group, and I've made a presentation that was given to my whole school year by the head of year. I'm organizing talks for the police force and ambulance service. There have been times when the police have asked if I'm drunk, and I've said, "No, I have disabilities." It's so important to make sure people in authority understand.

> ❝Something that makes me feel strong is spreading awareness about Tourette's. I've given presentations, and people have come up to me afterwards and they've said they've learnt a lot from me. I know a lot of them would have no idea about the condition if I wasn't giving talks.
>
> Talking in public doesn't always feel easy. I get quite anxious when I begin to speak, but when I get into it, the words just kind of flow naturally."

My old history teacher from year seven to nine was the best teacher I've had. He was the first teacher to make me feel normal. He ignored my tics, and if they were funny, he'd laugh with me. If he could see I was struggling, he'd come over and help me. When he moved schools, he asked me if he could take my presentation on Tourette's with him to help the staff there.

I'm part of Tourettes Action UK – a great charity that helps whole families. I've been chosen as one of their Champions, and we fundraise, put up posters, and spread the word. I've even been on a TV documentary.

I make friends at the Tourette's Camps that the charity runs. Even the staff have tics, and we all understand each other. We know we're just our normal selves.

My best friends are kind, and they don't care that I have tics. If I'm struggling, they ask what they can do to help me. Sometimes they distract me, or we go for a walk.

When I feel passionate about something, I feel really passionate about it. I think some of the best people I've met are other people who feel different; people who have disabilities. They are the people I've made the strongest connections with.

Schools must have patience with anyone with disabilities. Wellbeing must be a priority. If your mind is busy with negative thoughts, there's no way you're going to do your best in a lesson. Teachers need to be trained to look for signs that students are feeling overwhelmed, because sometimes they'll stay silent about it.

Time to reflect: What are good ways for a teacher to help a child who is feeling overwhelmed?

Parents may want their children to fit in with the normal, but they shouldn't try to make them a different person. It's better to research what's going on with them. Friends can help by not being embarrassed and not treating us differently. Also, they should stick up for us when we're vulnerable.

> "We need to remember, there are all these other people in the world going through the same things that we are. We need to find the people to be with that we're meant to find, even if that means being on our own for a while. We need good people.
>
> None of us should give up on what we want to do. That may mean struggling more than other people, but we can do it. We can use our inner strength. In the end we'll get there."

KAIS, 9, MERSEYSIDE, ENGLAND

My family moved from the war in Libya, where I was born, to Syria. In Syria there was another war, so we had to leave there as well, and we came here at the end of 2021. By that time, I had missed a lot of school because it had been too dangerous for me to go.

> **Time to reflect:** Imagine living through two wars when you are still a child! What would that be like?

I knew I was safe in England, but when I first came to this school, I was nervous that I might say or do something wrong, and people might be mad with me. My English wasn't good, and I had missed a lot of my education. Then someone asked me to be their friend. That was Charlie, who is still my best friend today. It's Charlie who's helped me the most since I've been here. He's made me feel included.

> **"**When people ask if you want to be their friend, it's like they're your family. I don't feel any different from the rest of them now, but when I did feel different, it helped me become a kind person and notice when other people feel left out."

One of my friends has a stammer when he speaks. Some people aren't kind to him because of that. We tell the

DIFFERENT LIKE US!

teachers, and they tell us not to let him go near those people. They say our friend should stay with us.

This means it's my job to help look after him. I feel like a really good friend.

My friends are good to me too. They bring me snacks and we play football together. If I feel sad, one of the things I always do is play football. My friends helped me learn English when I couldn't speak much at all. People would talk and I wouldn't understand the words. I started watching what they were doing and copying them to work out what they meant. From then on, I stopped being nervous and I've caught up with the others at school.

I once gave a talk to my whole school about my country, Syria. I told them about the capital city and what Muslims are and what Christians are. This helped them understand me and who I am. If anyone's mean to me now, it's not because I'm from somewhere else, it's just because that's what happens sometimes.

DIFFERENT LIKE US!

LUNA, 13, LONDON, ENGLAND

Everything sounds so loud to me that sometimes I wear moulded ear defenders to protect my ears. This especially helps at school where the background sounds distract me, causing me stress and anxiety.

I've been tested and I can hear sounds that are higher and lower than most people. If something's loud, the nerves in my ears can't cope. This makes my muscles freeze, and I can't move, which is not helpful if you need to get out of the classroom to find a place which is quiet and nice.

Feeling different at school makes me seem like the odd one out of the class. People ask me what the things are in my ears and pull at them, and I say, "You shouldn't do that." The anxiety makes me feel divided from everyone else, like there's a wall between us, with all these people giving me odd looks.

When I first went to secondary school,* the teachers at school were supportive. After a while they had to work on other things, but I felt I needed extra support the whole way through.

Because of the noise, I find it so hard to concentrate. I'm a twin, which means I have a super special best

---

* Aged 11

friend, but I am also different from my sister. She fits into the system, and I don't. Sometimes that gets me down. I have ADHD, dyslexia, and ASD* and she doesn't. I'm good at things outside the curriculum but that doesn't completely make up for not doing well at school. School takes up a lot of your life.

> **Time to reflect:** How would you feel about being a twin?

When my parents saw me struggling, they tried to help but they felt they couldn't. Nothing like this had happened in our family before. So I started seeing a therapist who did art therapy with me, which I liked. School helped too. They gave me a medical pass to give me time out from class if I needed it. In year seven I had stopped eating because I couldn't deal with the noise at lunchtimes, but in year eight** I was given a lunch pass, so I could go to lunch five minutes early. Now I eat at a SEN Lunch Club which is quiet. I have my own pupil passport to show what my needs are.

I think in years seven and eight*** every kid needs some kind of help, but not everyone wants to talk about how they feel. I don't even talk to my friends about feeling different. This means sometimes I feel lonely even with my friends, but no one should ever give up on their

---
* Autism Spectrum Disorder
** Seventh grade in the USA
*** Sixth and seventh grade in the USA

friends, even if they dip in and out of contact with them. They'll come round. We have a whole lifetime to feel better about ourselves.

> **❝I used to not tell anyone about my anxiety, but anxiety makes you learn things about yourself that you didn't know before. It's like a light bulb turning on. I learnt to believe in myself and be who I am.❞**

For a long time, I didn't want to tell anyone I had differences because I wanted people to treat me the same as everyone else. Now I put stickers on my books that say **be happy** and **don't worry**. I write down things that help me. I've had to teach myself that noise isn't always horrible. I've learnt to reach out for help and listen to every source of advice. My parents have helped me and other people have too.

Time to reflect: Do you think positive messages like the ones on Luna's books might help you when you feel down?

I'm learning you can feel positive about being different. I'm changing from feeling I don't want to show myself to knowing I can just be me. I don't need to feel scared about showing my ear plugs. If you hide yourself away, you feel unhappy. When you show yourself, you feel like yourself again.

My anxiety has gone down and I'm more confident. I used to hide my ears by wearing my hair down so people would forget, but I'm changing. I now wear my hair up all the time. I've decided it doesn't matter if you're different.

Key Question: How have you helped to change how other people think?

CHAPTER FIVE
RECEIVING HELP

DIFFERENT LIKE US!

JOSIE, 10, BATH, ENGLAND

A few weeks before school started, I was brought in and found out where everything was. My dad was with me and the teachers were there.

The school made sure my drawer was at the top of all the drawers so I can find it easily. My peg is at the end of the row, and my locker is above everyone else's. They've painted a line on the end of each step, so I can see where the steps are, and in class I always sit at the front.

One of my teachers explained about my eyesight to the whole class, and she said it was like putting your fingers in front of your eyes – that's how much I can see.

> **Time to reflect:** Imagine your life if you had problems seeing. What would you need to change? What would you need help with?

I'm allowed to take my iPad into assembly. This connects to the big screen so I can see what words are up there. They make the words bigger for me too. Some of our hockey balls are bright pink because this shows up more than white. Everyone always fights over the pink balls. We all want them! My maths sheets are A3 and yellow, instead of smaller and white. Once the teacher forgot to change the printer back to white paper, and everyone had yellow. They all said they liked it better.

One thing I don't like is that my two best friends have moved. One of them has gone to Hong Kong and the other is on holiday, but when she's back she's going to school in Bristol. I was very sad to say goodbye to them. They were always helping me, and I helped them as well in different ways. We all helped each other.

I'll need to make new friends now. There's a new girl starting in our class, and new people are the easiest to make friends with because they don't have any friends yet.

I think mine is a good school for anyone who can't see very well. It's friendly and the teachers are nice. Because of everything they've done for me, I don't feel that different from the others at school. My dog, Flora, is from the Guide Dogs charity. She helps me, and once she came in at playtime and everyone loved her.

I feel the same as the others when we do PE. I love PE. We do hockey, netball, and cricket. I can see well enough to know if someone is about to run into me. I try to run away – but it doesn't always work.

I find it difficult to recognize faces. The right side of my vision doesn't work as well as the left side. My teachers wear hi-vis jackets so I can recognize them easily. One non-uniform day the teachers didn't wear the special jackets and the year sixes* weren't in uniform, so I couldn't tell them apart from each other.

> "I like being able to express myself, and to show people I'm different but still amazing. Sometimes people don't even know I have a problem with my eyesight until the teacher tells them. When they realize, I think, "Oh, I've literally changed their life." It's a good feeling. I've taught them it doesn't matter if you're different.
>
> My mum says I'm a good listener because I can't see very well, and that my little brother's a good listener because he copies whatever I do, so that's a good thing too."

My mum and dad drive me to school, and sometimes they drop me off five minutes away and I walk the rest. I like doing that. I'm naturally a friendly person so I'm good at helping myself. My family, the Guide Dogs charity, and teachers have all helped me as well.

Every single little thing someone does to help makes a big difference. It's so important to be thoughtful. It's also important that friends treat you just the same as they always have. Because we are the same.

What's unhelpful is when I'm asking where something is and I say, "Where is it?", and they say, "Over there."

---

* Fifth grade in the USA

OK. That doesn't help me at all. I'm totally in the place I started with no information. They need to say, "On the windowsill" or "On the shelf in the kitchen." Something like that.

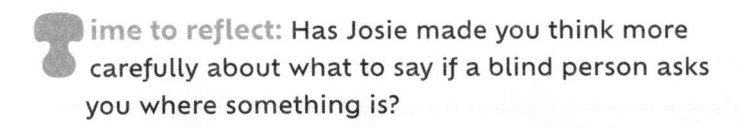

Time to reflect: Has Josie made you think more carefully about what to say if a blind person asks you where something is?

> "I think anyone who feels different should be proud. Every day you're teaching the world you're amazing. It might be harder to achieve some things, but if you know what you want to do, you can do it. Just keep being kind to everyone and looking on the bright side."

ROBYN, 10, LANCASHIRE, ENGLAND

Washing my hands became a habit because of Covid when we were all told to keep washing our hands. At school I washed my hands before breaktime, before I went into classes, and before lunch. Then after school I washed my hands again.

When they said we didn't need to keep washing our hands anymore, I carried on doing it anyway. I told myself the others at school didn't notice. I'm still doing it now. I don't say anything about handwashing to any of my friends, but knowing I do this, and I can't stop, does make me feel a bit separate from them.

I've been told I have OCD – obsessive compulsive disorder. As well as the handwashing, this means I keep saying words in my head. I can't watch YouTube videos and YouTube shorts once; I have to watch them three times. I have to say goodbye to the sink and the bathroom before I leave them. If I don't, I feel like I would explode. My brain would go crazy.

I get panicky when things aren't tidy because I need to know where stuff is. I worry that if we need to rush in the mornings because Mum has to be at work for a certain time, I won't be able to find anything.

I'm also sensitive to noise. I don't like assemblies because some of the others can be annoying and loud

DIFFERENT LIKE US!

RECEIVING HELP

and then my headteacher uses a loud voice too. I like things to be calmer.

> **Time to reflect:** Do you like the noise at school or do you prefer everything to be quieter?

If a teacher shouts a lot this gives me a shock and makes me panic. My teacher this year is kind and that helps me. I also don't like the busyness of school, when people in the corridors are screaming and I can't get through to my classroom because they are all in the way.

My teacher has given me a time-out card so that when someone shouts and I get overwhelmed, I can put the card on my desk and go out and come back again when I feel calmer. But I don't want people asking me where I went or what I'm doing. I've been moved to a desk next to the door, so if I do need to leave, I don't need to walk out in front of everyone, passing everyone's desks.

> **"**One of the best things that school has done for me is that they have given me mindfulness lessons with a special teacher on my own before school. These lessons calm me down a lot and help me focus. When I'm having these lessons, none of my rituals come into my mind – I don't need to do everything three times or be so tidy."

At school I do have good friends. They never leave me out and always ask me if I want to join in with what they're doing. I don't ever go to sleepovers though, as I wouldn't be able to do my rituals in someone else's house.

Sometimes I feel the same as the others at school. I love being part of the football team, just focusing on the game and nothing else. A lot of the rest of the time I feel different and separate.

My mum helps me, giving me advice. Sometimes it works, sometimes it doesn't. Sometimes I can help myself, pushing myself to ignore the voices in my head. That's when I'm at my strongest.

Time to reflect: How can you help yourself when you don't feel strong?

My school is good at listening to what helps me. Schools need to do that – to listen to what the children need. Parents need to stay strong for their children and be as patient as they can be. With OCD, it's not you that's doing the rituals, it's the voice in your head. It's so hard to ignore what that voice seems to be making you do.

> "No one who feels different needs to feel scared. Remember there are other people in the world who have what you have. They are dealing with it as well so you're not on your own. You're not the only one fighting what's happening to you.
>
> Do what you can to keep happy and spend time with people you like, doing things that you enjoy. We are much bigger than the things that worry us."

DIFFERENT LIKE US!

LORCAN, 10, LONDON, ENGLAND

I live with two mums – we call them Mum and Mammy – and, when I was in year three,* someone I hardly knew was rude to me about my parents in the playground. This was before there had been assemblies about homophobia. They didn't know much and just assumed things.

The amazing thing is that we're in the same class this year, and they came up to me and apologized. The two of us are now good friends.

> **I think this is a great example of what's so good about my school. After the other person was rude to me, the school did an assembly in the same week. They didn't mention what happened, but they did talk about what's OK to say and what's not OK."

I think if they hadn't done that, my friend wouldn't have apologized.

Time to reflect: Can you think of a time you've said sorry to someone and this has helped them to forgive you?

---

* Second grade in the USA

This makes me think that maybe in a different school, things might have been harder for me; if I'd been at a school where the teachers hadn't been so willing to act on what happened. Other schools should learn from my school.

Schools can do a lot to help children who feel different. They can celebrate International LGBTQ+ Day and Black History Month and hold assemblies to find ways to support anyone who needs it.

The other day my school organized a black cultural evening, with free food and face paint and dance. It was really fun. That's another example of how inclusive the school is. The teachers are really kind.

My friends are kind too. What I like about them is that they don't judge. If I'm doing or saying something embarrassing, they don't think any more or less of me. Maybe they tease, but only in a friendly way, giggling a bit but nothing rude.

Good friends are like that. They don't say anything that could even in the slightest way be hurtful about something you don't feel secure about. If they do, they apologize about it later.

Question: How would you react if a friend was mean to you?

Most of the time at school, I don't feel different from the others, but there are good things about being different. People might be more curious about you. They can ask you a question, and they won't think they'll get the same answer as they'll get from anyone else they've asked. All of this makes you a more interesting person.

> "I guess there's a chance that if you're different, you can have better, stronger friendships. In our family we have an experience most people don't have and that means we have something different we can give to other people. Also everyone's different in some way, so people can identify with you."

Although kids don't like long conversations with their parents, and I don't like them either, if something's troubling you, I think it's important to sit down with your parents and talk about whatever makes you feel different. Parents can help their kids feel better, as much as they can. It's a way of letting your children know you are there for them and a reminder not to hold things in that are upsetting you.

DIFFERENT LIKE US!

ABUBAKARR, 14, EASTERN REGION, SIERRA LEONE

When I was younger, I was begging in the streets. My parents couldn't support me because they are not financially strong. I wasn't happy – I'm blind, and people used to mock me and be mean. Of course, I couldn't see what they were doing and that made it worse.

Then something happened that changed my life. I made a friend who also has a visual impairment. She understood how I was feeling. She encouraged me to stop begging, and found me a shelter to live in. Here the roof leaks sometimes, but it is so much better.

My friend also found me a school place so I could be educated with others my age. Now I have a lot of joy in my life. I like singing, reading using braille, and dancing. School supports me, and they've put me in charge of composing songs and leading the singing during assemblies and school functions.

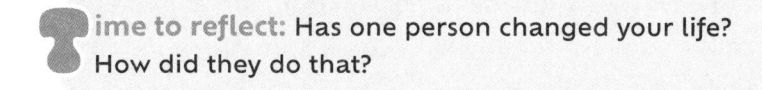

Time to reflect: Has one person changed your life? How did they do that?

At first I moved in with my auntie and uncle, but my auntie is so busy, she can't always help me get to school on time. This meant I was missing a lot of lessons, so it is better for me to stay in the shelter.

All of us at school are acquiring the same knowledge, but sometimes I think this is the only way that I'm the same as them. I can't take part in sport and some other activities because of my eyesight. Also the teachers write on the blackboard and I can't see this to copy it down. My friend gave me her old recorder to tape my lessons, so I can study them after school, but the recorder doesn't always work well, so I need a better one. These are the things that put me at a disadvantage.

The other students are kind to me and support me and I pray for them. I always try to encourage myself so that I will not feel unhappy. I see myself as a strong person in that way.

Sometimes if I'm sitting down and lonely at school and I'm not happy, my uncle, who works at the school, helps me. He asks me why I'm sitting alone. He talks to me and calls my friends over to come around and be with me.

I cannot see my classmates and they can see me, so that will always make me feel different, but I am still happy because I believe that I will become somebody in life at the end of my education.

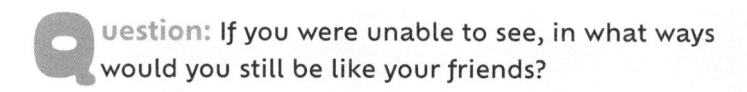

Question: If you were unable to see, in what ways would you still be like your friends?

RECEIVING HELP

My goal is to be a music artist. After writing a song, I go over and over it, again and again. In that way I'm able to study the music and memorize it and sing it.

Sightsavers helps me.* They work with my school, and give me the courage to do my best. They make me believe I can do what I want to do. One person from Sightsavers is my mentor. I explain my problems and challenges to him. I've told him I need a typewriter and a better recorder to help me get through my exams. Without the right equipment I can't do all the work.

> "Being blind has made me a stronger person. Although I cannot see, I always have the hope and faith that I will become a successful person in life. Being different has given me a determination. I know I will find a better shelter to live in one day. Then, after I finish my education, I think I will be able to find somewhere better still."

I miss my parents, but as I don't live with them, I have more interest in people who encourage me, like my uncle. I have learnt that if you don't have someone to encourage you, you will not be inspired to do what you want with life.

---

* For information on Sightsavers, see the section on support at the end of the book

> "I would say to anyone with a disadvantage that if you feel low like I did when I was begging in the streets, find someone to be friends with, or someone to support you and help you work out what your skills and talents are. Then you can achieve something that will make your nation admire you."

HUGH, 10, VICTORIA, AUSTRALIA

One thing that feels different about me is that I don't have a dad, I have a donor dad. This was because my mum wanted to have a child and hadn't met the right partner. I am also an only child, which is not common.

Mum explained to me when I was quite young that the doctor told her not all people have babies in the same way. She said I was conceived using sperm from someone she didn't know, organized by a doctor.

Some of my friends know about this, and they don't talk to me about it because they don't need to. They know not to make a big deal of it. They're good friends. The ones I haven't told don't know because I don't want them to go and tell other people.

So, at school, when some of my friends say, "Dads are the best," I join in and say, "Yeah, dads are the best," because I don't want them to know I don't have one.

Sometimes, when my mum comes and picks me up, and other kids are going home with their dads, they say to me, "Where's your dad?" I'll say, "He's at work," to avoid the conversation.

Time to reflect: When have you avoided difficult conversations?

DIFFERENT LIKE US!

RECEIVING HELP

Every year the school has a Father's Day Stall for Father's Day that we're allowed to buy something from. I always go and buy something for my grandpa and make a card.

School is good. I have some good teachers and I have a lot of friends in my class. I have dyslexia and one of my friends does as well, so it's not just me. Some of my friends help me with the things I find difficult, and I like it when we work together with a partner.

I don't like reading and maths, and the worst thing is when we have a CRT (Casual Relief Teacher). That's when our normal teacher is away sick, and someone new comes in for the day.

Usually I get easier work because of my dyslexia, but with a CRT you have to do the exact same work as all the others. If it's my usual teacher, when we do reading I can go out of the classroom to a place to read by myself and listen to books. With a CRT, I have to stay in class and do sight reading for a whole lesson and that doesn't help me.

If I ever hear someone say, "Oh this work is too easy for me," that made me feel a bit sad, even though I know there are things that I'm good at that they might not be.

My friends at school are great. We all like playing sports, kicking the soccer ball, playing cricket, or playing "gang up" – when somebody's **It** and they count to a certain number and we all go and run away, and if they tag you, you're both in it together, and the last one to be tagged wins.

I feel the same as the others when we all get the same work, and we only have to write one paragraph as that's not too much. I feel the same in art and PE, because I'm average and above average in them. That feels good.

I'm someone who cares about people and I'm good with younger children. All teachers should have more training so they can help more kids who find schoolwork difficult. Schools should also make sure they have different work for children who find school hard. If anyone's making fun of you, you should tell them to stop it and say you don't like it. If they keep on doing it you should tell a grown-up or your teacher.

Parents can buy their kids easier books to read. My mum does that. Also, parents shouldn't barge in and interrupt when we're about to speak, whenever I stop to breathe. Mum says she thinks I've finished what I wanted to say, but she should ask.

> "One positive thing about not having a dad is that I'm unique and that's a bit special. I'm close to my mum – we're a bit of a team, which is good sometimes and not so good at other times. I love my dog, Daisy, and I love throwing tennis balls for her. That's one of my favourite things. Sometimes if I have had a bad day Daisy can make me feel better and she makes me happy. If I haven't had a good day, it's my mum and my dog who have helped me the most."

Question: Is there an animal in your life that helps you feel better, and how do they do that?

DIFFERENT LIKE US!

VIKTORIIA, 8, UKRAINE AND MERSEYSIDE, ENGLAND

Coming to a country where they speak a different language is hard because you don't always understand what's going on. In fact, when I first arrived, I didn't understand anything. I felt different from everyone.

The school gave me a lanyard to wear that had different words on it to tell people when I needed to translate something, when I felt upset, or when I needed the toilet.

> **Question:** Can you think of ways you would help someone who spoke a different language?

That's just one way the school has helped me. They've helped me learn English and feel part of the community. Now I can understand much more, and I can explain to my mum what the school asks for when they send letters home.

My friends here are kind to me. They always help when I need them to. They talk to me more slowly to make sure I know what they're saying and that makes me feel special and that they care about me.

All my family except my dad and my mum are in Ukraine. My brother is there – he's 20. My grandparents are there. I am worried about them and think about how they are because of the war there. This makes me different from the others in my class. My friends don't know I worry about this, but my teacher knows.

> "Some things are good about feeling different. I know what life is like in two different countries, the habits, customs, and costumes. I have much more experience than other English children – I know how to speak two languages, I know for sure that people in different countries think differently, and that their way of life is different. I have even been able to teach my classmates to speak Ukrainian. That was very funny."

I am very happy that I study at this school. All the teachers and children who are here made me very welcome and accepted me. I feel like I am in a fully-fledged family. It is thanks to them that I understand a lot in English now, and I am starting to behave like an English girl.

RECEIVING HELP

MIA, 7, OKLAHOMA, USA

I have asthma and an allergy to dairy. I had back surgery when I was a baby. They said at some point, I might be paralysed from the waist down and end up in a wheelchair. If so they will operate again. I can walk, run, and play now but sometimes my back hurts if I do too much of that stuff. It feels like it's burning up. If I run too much, I start wheezing with asthma. So, if my cousins are playing football, I play a little bit, then I stop and sit that out.

> "The good thing about being different is that people help me out. If I tell people I have asthma, I feel nervous because I want to be the same as them, but if they don't have a problem with it, I feel fine. If I need it, my friends get me my asthma treatment. If I'm sitting out instead of playing sport, a friend will ask me if there's something they can do, and I say yes."

Key Question: What are the different ways you can get help?

DIFFERENT LIKE US!

CHAPTER SIX
MAKING ME STRONGER

DIFFERENT LIKE US!

AIDAN, 13, CUMBRIA, ENGLAND

My dad died when I was five, so I don't have many memories of him now. I remember one time walking into a theme park, Thomas Land, with him and I remember us watching football on the telly. That's about it.

> **"** If anyone brings up fatherhood at school, that's when I feel different. Most people know all sorts of stuff about their fathers, and I don't. If people are talking about who they live with at home, I think, 'I don't have that person there when I go home. Most of the class will.'"

That's when I keep quiet and avoid eye contact. I kind of sink into my chair and don't listen to what people are saying to try to take my mind off whatever's being said.

Every year we buy Dad a Father's Day card and take it to his grave. Mum always walks away and lets me have a few minutes there by myself. We also visit him on birthdays, Christmas, and the anniversary of his death. I think this helps me. I know part of Dad is there and I feel connected to him.

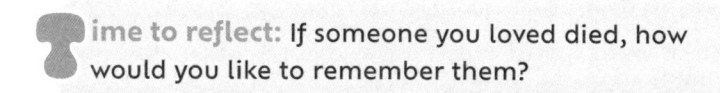

Time to reflect: If someone you loved died, how would you like to remember them?

I live with my mum, my stepdad Leigh, and my stepbrother Harrison. Leigh does things with me my dad would have done, like showing me DIY. He tries to include me.

I have great friends who are funny, and I love having a laugh with them. My best friend Abbie's mum died recently. We talk about this together easily. I know I've helped them and they listen to me.

My dad died after he had a blood clot in his brain. That's what caused him to have a stroke. After that he found it hard to move, speak, or swallow. All of this happened out of the blue. I was on a trip to Scotland with my mum and sister. Dad was rushed to hospital, and they were trying to get hold of us. At one in the morning on the Saturday night, my grandma reached my mum who scooped up me and my sister and we drove down to the hospital.

When we saw Dad, I was scared because his speech was so different, so he gave me a thumbs up to put my mind at rest. That was on the Sunday. He died the next day.

I am lucky my mum is easy to talk to. Fairly recently I've been asking her more questions because there are gaps in what I can remember. That's why we've been in touch with Child Bereavement UK. We go there every couple of weeks, and they help me cope with what I can remember and what I can't. Talking to Abbie also helps me and talking to my big sister.

> "Sometimes I think of Dad in my day-to-day moments. I want to be an actor, and if I have a script in front of me that I have to learn in a certain amount of time and I nail it, I think he would be proud.
>
> Dad played a bit of rugby, and when I was playing today, I was thinking about him looking down on me which pushed me to try harder.
>
> I feel confident when others talk about people dying. It makes you realize how common grief is, and because of what I've been through I can talk about it more easily. What I've experienced has given me a certain knowledge that I'd rather not have but it's still useful in some situations.
>
> There's also a strength in knowing that I won't let the memories get me down. At some stage I know I will get on with my life."

Schools must make sure kids who are different for any reason feel included, not left out. We're part of the conversation. We're part of the place and have the right to be here, not different from anyone else. Schools need to acknowledge they know what we're going through and that this doesn't stop us learning, talking, and having fun.

I think parents should ask their children how they're feeling and, if they say "OK", then ask again if they're sure they feel OK. Sometimes that second question can trigger more of a conversation.

I want everyone to know that it's OK to feel different from other people. Everyone has their differences in their own way. You're not the only one with those feelings in that place, at that time. Never be afraid to share your feelings and open up. No one has the right to judge.

GEORGE, 11, GREATER MANCHESTER, ENGLAND

Diabetes doesn't control my life. I don't let it take over. I'm more like, "I'm George. Here's loads of stuff about me… And, oh yeah, I have diabetes."

At my primary school* I was the only student with type one diabetes, but someone who worked there had it too, and that made me feel like I wasn't different.

Then she left and that made me more aware of not wanting to be different, but I was too busy messing around with my mates at school to worry. It was after school, when I was sitting on the couch watching TV, that my mind would go off in another direction. I was about to go to high school,** and I didn't want to get bullied there or feel like I wasn't fitting in.

I had a good chat about this with my mum and she contacted the charity Diabetes UK. They have a regional section where we live, and they put me in touch with this amazing youth worker called Josh. We had a Zoom call, and he was really friendly. He broke down any barriers very quickly and gave me the chance to ask any questions I wanted.

---

* Elementary school in the USA
** Middle school in the USA

DIFFERENT LIKE US!

MAKING ME STRONGER

Josh runs groups for 11–18-year-olds to put kids and young people with diabetes in touch with each other. The first thing I did with the group was go roller skating. Josh has diabetes himself and I love the way he puts funky stickers on his Dexcom – that's his continuous glucose monitor. I have one of those monitors too. It sends readings about my glucose levels directly to my phone, and I can check this whenever I want to, even at school. An alarm goes off if it's low, and an alarm goes off if it's high.

> **Time to reflect:** Why do you think it might be helpful to talk to others with the same condition as you?

I love sport, which is lucky because sport's good for you if you have diabetes. I love everything to do with rugby, football, basketball, all sports. I love playing them and watching them. In fact, I enjoy most things apart from tidying my room and washing the dishes. I'll get involved with anything.

I started high school in September. I have great friends, and I walk to school with two of them. They're always there for me and know all about me.

I watch what I eat at school and the rest of the time as well. I want to stay healthy so it's important for me. I give myself insulin if I'm high, and glucose if I'm low.

The amount of insulin I need is based on the carbohydrate count for my meals. So a jacket potato would be a high carb meal, a chicken salad is a low carb meal. I give myself the insulin based on the number of carbs I've eaten.

Almost all the time I feel the exact same as everyone else at school now. No different at all.

> "I do think feeling different can benefit me though – when I captain the football team, it gives me a real push and drives me forwards. It gives me another reason to do well that others haven't got.
>
> As well as sport, another strength of mine is my ability to put my head down and do whatever I need to do. I know how to turn a negative into a positive. It's who I am."

I'm also someone who puts my friends and family first. Mum says I'm dependable and caring and my friends say, "You're one of the biggest lads I have ever known, but you're one of the nicest." Looking out for other people is something I've always done. That's the way I've been brought up, to look out for people when they need it. If someone does something silly or says something nasty or a bit odd or acts out of character, I will always check they are OK before anything else.

My mum has helped me more than anyone with my diabetes. I couldn't ask for a better mum. If I've had a bad day she just knows. She's always there for me.

If I'm ever on the verge of giving up on something, she'll be like, "No, you don't give up."

Question: Who would you turn to first if you needed some support?

Schools need to keep a look out for anyone who feels different in any way. Once when I could feel my glucose levels were too low, I said to my mate Aaron, "I'm low," and I didn't need to say anything else. He bolted off to tell his teacher. You need to have those people around you who make you feel like you belong.

Anyone who feels different needs that support. They should speak to people they trust and that will help them sort things out for themselves or take action to feel better.

> "Everyone's different in their own way. Everyone's unique. We all need support to bring out the best in ourselves."

For me it's sport that helps. Rather than sitting down and playing on an Xbox, it keeps me active and keeps my blood sugars down. Maybe if someone has a different sort of difference, having a hobby would take them away from what worries them too. Maybe this will make them feel better about themselves and take them away from difficult feelings. Worth a try.

DIFFERENT LIKE US!

TAMALA, 14, CENTRAL REGION, MALAWI

Instead of living with my mum, I live with my aunt. Some of the others at school tease me about this. They ask me where my mother lives but they're not asking me because they're interested. They just wait until I tell them, then they say rude things about her that aren't true.

My mum lives in her home village with my older brothers and sisters. They have dropped out of school, but I'm still finishing my education. This is why she sent me to live with her sister – my mum felt it would be best for me and help me do well and school is important in Malawi so we can try to get good jobs. On the other hand, my life can be difficult. My mum didn't mean this to happen, but I feel disadvantaged. I know my friends' parents monitor their school progress closely, but my mum is too far away to check on mine, so I feel left out and less motivated.

> **Time to reflect:** How would you feel if you moved away from home?

My mother supports me any way she can, by paying for some of my necessities like my uniform, while my aunt pays for my exercise books.

> **❝** My friends at school care about me and are kind to me, but some of the others in my class are meaner. The only good thing about this is that when they are mean, it makes me want to do well in class. It's one of the reasons I work hard at school. I don't want to feel trapped like this when I'm older. I want to grow up to be an independent woman. When I go out to work, I want to be a pilot. I'm determined.
>
> So sometimes I feel sad because I'm not getting looked after by my mum like the others, but I also use the way I'm treated as a motivation to drive me and make me stronger.
>
> I think anyone who feels different at school should react by working harder and showing the others what they can achieve. That's the best way to get back at anyone who is harsh to you."

Going to girl guides helps me as well, as it gives me time to take part in drama and music which I love and make me feel better. The leaders at girl guides also teach us to report any gender violence – this is a big problem in Malawi – and this empowers us. My friends help me too by being kind. The best thing about school is chatting to them and helping to show them the way to succeed in their lives. We support each other.

GRACIE, 13, SOMERSET, ENGLAND

When I'm older I want to be a primary school teacher. I've had so much support from my school, I want to give something back and pass on good things to others who are struggling.

The staff at my school help students individually, but they also do a lot of assemblies on things like anti-bullying, and I think that helps everyone.

> **“**At school I have my "triangle of trust", which is made up from three main teachers and I know I can go to them if I needed them. The most important thing schools can do is never give up on the child in their care.”

Twice a week I go to an art therapy club at lunchtime run by one of the teachers. This is for a group of children who've been invited who have difficulties at home or at school. We have music on in the background, and all sorts of different activities to try, including colouring, pasting, and sticking.

I'm in this group because my dad's in prison, and also because I'm neurodiverse, and I'm in the process of being assessed at the moment. Being there helps me express myself and understand how I'm feeling.

DIFFERENT LIKE US!

I have counselling sessions that are available on a Tuesday lunchtime when external counsellors come into school, and they have a drop-in so you can see them if you think it will help. This is all great support for anyone who needs to be listened to and understood.

Something else that's good for me is that I have friends in all my lessons. This helps because I'm not exactly antisocial, but I don't like making new friends because I think I'm autistic. It makes things so much easier that I have friends in every class.

My friends are all supportive. They make me laugh at least once every day. In art, I've got a whole table which is basically my whole friendship group, and it's always fun being with them.

I think I'm the only person at school with a parent in prison. When it comes to talking about our parents in class, it does get a bit awkward because there's nothing I can say about my dad. This weekend some of my friends were talking about what they'll do with their dads, and I don't have that.

> **"No one at school knows what's happened with Dad so I don't ever get to talk to anyone about it. This means I'm not included in the conversations. I can't talk about what I've done with my dad, and I can't talk about where my dad is. I'm doubly not included."**

The reason I've not told anyone about my dad is that I know the way rumours spread around and get twisted. I don't want that to happen, though good friends should never pass on anything they're told in confidence.

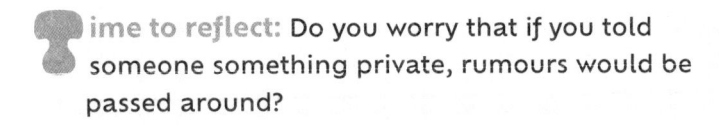

Time to reflect: Do you worry that if you told someone something private, rumours would be passed around?

I've never lived with my dad, I used to see him every weekend but now I'm not allowed to see him in prison or have any contact with him.

At other times I feel the same as the others at school. A lot of my friends have ADHD and autism, though across my wider group some of them don't. A lot of them have a similar personality to me and are very talkative. When I'm in lessons I don't stop talking unless I get told to stop. It's quite a happy feeling to feel the same as my mates, and there are definitely some positives about feeling different. I think I have more of an understanding of other children who feel different and maybe I'm more compassionate because of that.

I have strong bonds with children who have one of their parents in prison. I went to a weekend group organized by Children Heard and Seen* that looks out for children

---

* For information about Children Heard and Seen, see the section on support at the end of the book

who have parents in prison, and I connected with a group of children I might never even have met before. Some of them were as young as four or five and some were as old as 18.

Time to reflect: If you were facing a difficult situation, would it help you to talk to others who were going through the same thing?

> "My teachers tell me I'm someone who doesn't give up. I keep on trying no matter how difficult things are. I went into school the day after my granddad passed and that was tough, but I still did it. I think I've built up my strength, thanks to support from Mum and my whole family and the school. I find my own ways to calm myself too. Colouring in at night is one thing that helps me wind down and face the next day.
>
> I believe children who are going through difficulties should speak to a trusted adult in their lives. As well as that, everyone should find friends who make them laugh, people who make them happy. Also, find your favourite thing to do, that's special to you and makes you feel special. You have so much to offer. Even when times are hard, now is the time to make the best of your life."

DIFFERENT LIKE US!

SIENNA, 10, KENT, ENGLAND

Everyone thinks I'm treated like the special kid in the class because I have to leave to go to counselling during the day, or it's time for me to go to see one of the other teachers.

None of the others in my class knows why this is. Some people think it's because I have asthma and go to a clinic. I don't know what everyone else thinks. I tell them that I have something important to go to, something private that only people in my family are allowed to know.

The real reason I leave the class is that my dad is in prison, and I have support to help me deal with this from different people and organizations.

> **❝** It doesn't feel good being different, knowing everyone else is going to be thinking something about me, knowing that I'm always leaving the class. I don't want to be seen as the favourite. I just want to be normal. I have my SATs to be working for as well so I shouldn't be missing my work."

One thing I go to is a support group where I do arts and crafts and spend time with other children in the same situation as me. I have support from a group called

Family Matters, and from this fantastic organization called Children Heard and Seen. I also see a counsellor.

> "All of this helps me because at school I don't think anyone else is in the same situation as me, so I feel different from all of them. Only a few teachers know my real situation. In these other places I go to, the children feel the same as me, and people understand me."

One good thing about being different is that no one can blame me for anything because I'm not there, like if something goes wrong when my friends are playing football, it's definitely not my fault if I'm somewhere else.

Being different has helped me build up close relationships with two of my teachers as well, who I trust. It helps to talk to people like that.

Maybe what I'm going through has helped me be a more caring person. It was my mum's birthday yesterday and my dad obviously couldn't plan anything for her, so I did. I got all the family to WhatsApp her at the same time in the morning and we all sang happy birthday. I sent her a card. I wrote on it that I knew she didn't want to celebrate, but I told her to keep being powerful like she always is. I think all the groups I'm in help me understand other people's situations and their feelings. You get good at listening.

> **❝I have become stronger as a person. When people are rude to me in class, I've got better at telling them to stop. Once I was worried about something and I kept it to myself. Then I finally told my mum about it, and when I did, it felt amazing. I knew she understood and was on my side.**
>
> **I've decided that schools should set up an after-school club so all kids who feel different from the others can meet up with each other. We could all support each other. We could pass on all the things that helped us feel better."**

Lots of things have helped me, including talking to my teachers and my mum, and drawing some of my feelings in my art book. Something else that's helped is meeting up with people who feel the same as me, not always seeing the same people I always see at school.

Time to reflect: Does it help to have different friends outside school as well as your schoolfriends?

I've found out that one thing that helps if you're upset is to find a way to distract yourself. Staying tuned in to that for as long as you can help bad feelings to stop.

If my friends are being horrible, I just say no to them and that I don't like them behaving like that, but my best friends don't behave in that way. I can tell them anything and they won't pass it on. It's so important to know people who are on your side.

> "We have a sensory room at school to calm us and take us away from anything we want to escape from. At home I listen to Anne Marie and other music, and light candles with my mum. There are so many ways we can calm ourselves down."

Key Question: How do any of your differences make you stronger?

CHAPTER SEVEN
FINDING THE POSITIVES

DIFFERENT LIKE US!

RIYA, 11, LONDON, ENGLAND

When we don't have enough food or money at home, my life is stressful. I live with my mum and sister who have learning difficulties, my brother who has seizures, and my other brother who also has problems. My dad used to live with us, and he was working, but he moved out and he has a new wife now. We don't see him very often.

Even though I'm the youngest it's me who has the most responsibility. I'm the one who has to sort out anything that goes wrong. All the others see me as brave, independent, and smart, but sometimes it would be nice just to be looked after like other kids are.

Time to reflect: Would it be tough to have so much responsibility when you are young?

My mum's first language is Punjabi. She understands English but she gets her words jumbled up. So if we get letters, I have to read them to her and explain them to her because I know she won't understand them. I have to deal with all the bills and any other problems we're facing.

If my brothers ask my mum something, she tells them to ask me. One of my brothers can get mad easily. Then that's a load of stress on my mum and then the stress is passed on to me when she tells me to throw him out, but I can't because I'm close with him. It's hard because he's older and harder to take care of.

I know the others I'm at school with don't live like this.

> **❝With no money, life is difficult. I'm hungry most of the time and it's hard to focus on lessons. When we're out of money, we go to the food bank which can help, but some of the food goes off quickly so we don't eat it. That especially happens with the milk and bread. Then we have to wait for my child benefit to come in and I can get the essentials with that."**

School gives me the chance to come in and have breakfast, but because of the stress on me in the day, I don't get enough sleep at night. Then, I get to sleep in the early morning, and I don't wake up on time for the food they give out.

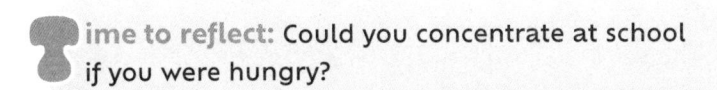

Time to reflect: Could you concentrate at school if you were hungry?

The other thing I feel I miss out on is clothes, and anything else I might want besides food. I sometimes hear the others at school talking about buying things I can never afford, but mainly I see kids on the street wearing better clothes than me, and I know they're not hungry at school like I am. I love make-up and want to be a make-up artist when I'm older. I'd love to buy more make-up to practise with.

> "One of the staff at school helps me. She takes me out of lessons, and we talk. I guess it means I can get things off my chest. It feels good to know that someone else knows what position I'm in. Everyone should have a trusted adult in school who they know they can talk to. That's the most important thing. Siblings are important too. They might understand you better than your mum. They're like a younger or older version of you."

I'm scared to tell other people at school, like my friends, about what my life is like. I don't want them to tell more people and then more people will find out. There is one girl who's much older who I talk to more. In our generation, if people know you don't have money you will get bullied or made fun of, but if you do have money, you can be told you're showing off, so both are hard.

The way I'm living now makes me think when I'm older I want to live differently. I hope to have a successful life and get a job and support the family. And I don't want my future kids to have to be in my situation. I'm determined to do well at school and in life.

> "Those of us who feel different need to keep doing what we're doing, because we're in a position that nobody else can understand, but we're getting through it. I have confidence in myself that I can do everything I need to do. We all need to have faith and believe in ourselves.
>
> The one good thing about my situation is that everything I'm going through makes me think that when I'm older, there's nothing I won't be able to deal with."

DIFFERENT LIKE US!

THIAGO, 10, MERSEYSIDE, ENGLAND

I have a condition called Neurofibromatosis type 1, or NF1 for short. This means I have tumours growing inside me that can't be fully removed. Once I asked the school if I could talk about this in assembly, and I did – in front of the whole school. I wanted to help others understand my condition better. I thought that way they could find out things they didn't want to ask me before.

I was a bit scared before I started but I told them about my disability, what happens when I wake up, and what my day is like. They were interested and asked me some questions.

> "I told them all about the surgeries that I've had and that I can't eat for many hours before I have my operations. When I wake up from the operation it hurts where the surgery has happened, and I feel very hungry and thirsty. At the end I had a big cheer. I felt like a superhero!"

Time to reflect: How would you feel if you were asked to talk to the whole school in assembly?

My school is a Rights Respecting school. This means

it's part of a special scheme that means everyone is respected. If you're disabled, you don't get treated differently. That makes me feel happy – not only because I'm included but because everyone else is as well.

Most of the time I feel the same as the others at school, but there are some things that make me feel different. I can do some PE but not all PE. If we're on a school trip, there are some activities I can't take part in for my own safety. I'm not allowed to go on rollercoasters in case I hurt my legs, and I can't go bungee jumping.

It's hard for me to walk because the tumours make one of my legs much bigger and heavier, so I have to drag it along or use my wheelchair. I have special footwear, to give me support. It's annoying that I can't run as fast as the others.

If I ever feel sad or in a grumpy mood, my friends notice, and they keep me company. They're kind whenever I fall over. They always check if I'm OK.

> "Most of the time, I feel happy that I'm different. It means I get asked different questions and people are curious about me. I like having that attention."

I miss school when I'm in hospital, but I'm used to it now. The doctors and nurses know me. My surgeon says there's a girl he operates on who has what I have. One day I'd like to meet up with her and talk about it with her.

Mum has helped me a lot. She helps me with pretty much everything. She makes sure places we go are suitable for my wheelchair and organizes my medicine and everything else I need.

Mum also tells me I'm "resilient". She says this means I'm like an elastic band that gets stretched and then bounces back. I can go through a lot and afterwards, when I've got over it, I feel OK. I go back to being me.

> **Question:** Are you ever like an elastic band, feeling stretched when things are hard, then bouncing back and feeling fine?

My dad had the same condition as me, and he died seven years ago. I miss him a lot. I go to his gravestone sometimes and talk to him. When we've finished planting flowers, we sit there in silence for a while.

We also have a little garden in our own garden at home with his picture and flowers on and a bench so I can sit and talk to him anytime I want.

> "I know I have to do some things differently from other people, but no matter how different we all are, we are all still human. We are all the same.
>
> No matter how much pain we have, the quicker we get through it, the stronger we get. That's how I see things. We need to find ways to clear our mind of the things that hurt us most."

T, 13, LONDON, ENGLAND

At my last school I was bullied badly. It got to the point where I was scared to walk to school or even leave the house. There were a lot of people being pushed against walls in the corridors, and a lot of trans-related slurs. I hated the noise and the crowds, and it was all too much for me.

I couldn't focus on my work, and my mental health was quite bad. Sometimes I couldn't go to school. I'd stay at home in my room and not come out without crying.

Then I moved school, and this one feels so much better. It's a far more accepting place, and I know there are people I can go to for help if I need it.

I've learnt a lot from both of these experiences. I think there is a very small percentage of people in this world who are properly bad, evil people. Anyone else causing trouble is either swayed by other people's decisions, or how they were brought up, or they are just trying to fit in. I believe they're all still good people underneath, but they need to make the choice to grow into that better person. They need to make the effort.

There are always going to be idiots and I don't want to waste time getting involved with them. It's taken me a while to get to this place of contentment, and I'm not going to give it up.

When I feel anxious now, I don't see it as the school's fault. I see it as something that I personally need to work on by myself. Schools are always going to be rowdy. That's just the way it's going to be.

At my new school I've met some like-minded people that I couldn't find anywhere else. I am so, so lucky to have moved. Some people here are still bad about transgender issues, but I think that's just the current time.

When you're a trans child, especially living in this world, just wanting to do anything as the gender that you are is very difficult. I was walking home, listening to music, and this group of boys from another school started shouting the T slur. They kept going, "Are you a boy or a girl?" They think they can be rude about a person and assume something about them that is very personal.

This may sound dramatic, but I said to my friend the other day that it's kind of like we're political soldiers now. We have to have each other's backs because otherwise nothing's going to get better.

Time to reflect: Who are the friends you feel you can truly trust?

At school I use the disabled bathroom, but I'm quite lucky with that because I don't want to use the boys, one as it's a bit gross. I get changed for PE in there too, and then have my PE class with the boys. It would be quite upsetting to be in the girls' PE class when you know that you're not one.

> **❝One wonderful thing in my life is my friends.** They have always been there for me when I've needed them most. They listen and make me laugh and we talk about my really obscure interests. They introduce me to new things that I would have never ever found before meeting them. They've listened to things that I've struggled with, because I need to talk out loud to process how I feel before creating solutions and plans for myself. They've taught me a lot about how to react to bad situations."

I imagine everyone in my position has that split second of thinking, "Ah, maybe I shouldn't do any of this. I should just sit in a hole forever," but I think it's better to live outwardly as who you are than have to crush who you are within yourself. If you do that, life is just going to be miserable, and if people want to isolate me or make me feel upset about who I am, then they're not worth listening to. That's their own problem.

I often feel the same as the others at school. It doesn't need to have anything to do with gender or being transgender. It can just be that we like the same things, we watch the same movies, or we can talk about a specific book. There's a sense of belonging that comes with that, but none of this should get in the way of knowing how unique you are, and that you're your own person, because that is special.

> ❝Being different is largely a good thing. It can make you feel really lonely, but once you find the people that you're comfortable being with and you find that feeling of being comfortable in yourself, that's all that will ever matter. Being different is being yourself, it's the journey to self-acceptance. I think I wouldn't be where I am today if it was not for the struggles I've faced."

If I feel troubled, going out for a walk by myself is a good way to escape. It gives me time to talk to myself about the emotions I'm going through. Listening to music also helps – it's my comfort thing. I feel like I've helped myself a lot, but my parents and my best friend have stuck by me through a lot of bad times.

Time to reflect: How do you help yourself feel better?

Schools need to listen to what their students need, and then be ready to change how they do things to accommodate them. Anxiety is never a useful base for learning your subjects. If you don't enjoy learning you're less likely to do well. Parents need to prioritize their children's needs too, and give time to listen and talk things through, and make changes to whatever needs to be changed.

> "I want everyone who feels different to know that, however hard it's going to be for them, they are loved, and that their differences should be celebrated. As much as life can sometimes feel awful, things can look up. They deserve that so much."

Note: If you are being bullied or know someone who is and want to help them, call Childline in the UK on 0800 1111. In the USA call the Stop Bullying Now Hotline on 1-800-273-8255.

DIFFERENT LIKE US!

198

CAITLYN, 12, OKLAHOMA, USA

I live with a brother and three sisters who all have medical conditions. It does make things harder for me. To get ice cream takes 30 minutes even to get in the car, because of all the medical equipment my brother Joey needs.

I like living in a family with all different kinds of kids because I like being the leader at home. I like doing the cooking and doing surprises for the family. I had already bought my Christmas presents at the beginning of November.

The attention at home isn't so much on me, but I make sure I do the things I want to do. That's important to me. One thing I do is rescue gerbils. So far I've rescued gerbils from five different states. One lady adopted two gerbils and found out they were a boy and girl and they had lots of babies. I went to get them and found homes for them. Some we look after in our house.

DIFFERENT LIKE US!

ISAAC, 12, NORWICH, ENGLAND

For anyone whose brother or sister has any kind of medical condition or disability, like my sister has, I think it's important to try to find the benefits. Work out the way that they have a positive impact on your life.

If anything in life feels too much, then try to move away from it and find something else to get lost in. There's always a way of doing that.

I take a positive approach in life. I believe in taking everything in my stride, not constantly worrying.
I always think, "Cross that bridge when you come to it," rather than spending time worrying about the future.
I see a bigger picture.

DIFFERENT LIKE US!

APRIL, 8, NEWCASTLE, ENGLAND

I was born with two rare conditions. One is tuberous sclerosis. This means that I get growths on my face, heart, and brain. The second is fibrous dysplasia, which means my bones are different shapes from usual. This is why my face looks different from a lot of people's.

We found this out because when I was a baby, my mum and dad noticed that I had different coloured eyes. They took me to the doctors to check my eyesight was OK. The doctor said my eyesight was good, but he found out about the other things.

> "I have to go to hospital quite a lot, and I don't like going. The great thing is my sister bought me a teddy called Mr Donut, who comes to hospital with me every time I have to go. The beds have the names of animals above them. Mr Donut sleeps in zebra bed. He's really cute. Little things like that make me feel better."

I have two sisters and a brother and they're all older than me. I like being the youngest because I get lots of attention from everyone.

There are also lots of things I love to do. I love playing football, especially winning and scoring goals. I used to go to a football club at weekends, but I got too tired, so I stopped that. I still play at school. I also went to True Colours, a club for children with disabilities, and I performed on stage when I was there. I had to stop doing the dance class because it hurt my arms and legs, and it hurt my throat when I was singing. What's the point of having a weekend if you get too tired or you start hurting? I'm always going to look after myself.

Another thing I love to do is fundraising for Changing Faces, the charity that helps us. At Easter I raised £1400, selling cakes and other things. I get bored easily, but I love doing this. It makes me feel like I'm doing something important and everyone's joining in with me.

Question: If you were going to raise money for a charity, which one would it be? How would you feel about yourself afterwards?

At school I like playing with my friends, especially Scarlet, Dillon, and Henry. Me and Henry used to be naughty in nursery school, chatting too much on the carpet, until the teacher stopped us.

Me and Scarlet are like twins. She's nice to me and we like the same things. There's nothing we don't like about school. We're very good at making each other laugh.

I like doing maths tests best. I love the way the numbers work together. Every school report has said that about my maths. Not everyone likes maths I know, but every single person loves different types of work. You just have to know which one is the one that's good for you.

My hearing isn't so good now, so I wear a hearing aid. This doesn't stop me playing.

I walk to school with Dillon every day. I play trains with Henry. He opens the door, and you get in, and sometimes when I don't play with him, he opens the door for invisible people to climb in. That's so funny.

> "Although I look different, I don't feel different. Mum says that's because I am so confident. The kids at school are the ones I grew up with. They just see me as April. When I go into high school* that will be another situation as lots of children there won't know me. I'll have to see what that's like when I'm there.
>
> The way I see it, if everyone was the same the world would be very boring. Having a difference makes you a kinder person. The best thing I've ever done is helping other people. I've helped my friends and I've raised money for charity.
>
> I think no one should ever be horrible to anyone else. If they're with someone who looks different, they should help them if they need it and never be mean.
>
> Remember, everyone looks different, but everyone is beautiful."

* At age 11

DIFFERENT LIKE US!

HUGO, 12, BUCKINGHAMSHIRE, ENGLAND

> "Parents and teachers should let children speak first and hear what they're trying to say. The biggest mistake they make is to decide they know what we're thinking.
>
> If someone wants to understand us well, they should just listen. That's all they need to do. They want us to listen, but it gets us more frustrated. It's easier if you just let us talk."

Having said that, my mum is definitely the person who helps me most. She's good at explaining things to me. If we go out in the car, before we leave I like to know how long the journey will take, how long we'll be out, and what time we'll be back. All of that is important to me and she understands that.

She's done other things that have helped, like having pictures on the fridge and the wardrobe with my uniform and medicine and lunch bag on them, so I don't forget anything in the mornings.

My friends are good at understanding me too. I've known them for so long they don't expect me to be anything except who I am. They know all about me.

At school I get treated differently by some of the teachers.

I'm autistic and I have ADHD and I have tics such as blinking a lot which we've been told are symptoms of Tourette's. I'm given extra help. Sometimes they give me help when I don't need it because I've understood the lesson anyway. I have a time out card that I'm allowed to use if I need to leave the class, plus a toilet card and a queue jump for lunchtimes, so I don't need to wait with everyone else. There's a lot of pushing and noise in the queue which I don't like, and the card keeps me away from it.

I don't mind feeling different. My friends aren't at my high school,* and I find it hard to make new friends now I'm there. I like being by myself, even at home. Sometimes my brother and sister are too loud for me and then everything kicks off a bit.

Time to reflect: Do you like to be quiet by yourself sometimes, or do you always like being with others?

The only class at school that's fun is PE and that's the time I feel the same as the others. I'm good at PE. One thing that's great about those lessons is that they can't give me extra help, so I'm not singled out. One week I have PE three days in a row, the next week I only have it once in the whole week, which is annoying.

---

* Aged 11 upwards in the UK

> **"** As I said, I don't mind feeling different most of the time. It's good to be different because no one's the same as anyone else. We are all unique people.
>
> If anyone gets to you or tries to cause trouble, walk away from them, and tell someone you trust what's going on. That's the best thing to do."

Key Question: What are the best things about being different?

Well, What Did You Think?

So many of the children and young teenagers in this book have lived through tough experiences, yet they have come through the other end strong and determined, living their lives in the best way they can. They are role models for others, a truly positive influence on the world around them.

For many, the ability to express themselves and ask for what they need has helped them get through some difficult times.

We are becoming more open – when it feels right

I had a great conversation with Catherine Woolley who works for STAMMA, the UK national charity for people who stammer, their friends, families, and those who support them.

She believes today's generation of young people are

talking more openly about what makes each of us different. She says exploring our differences in this way helps us as a society to understand and accept everyone more than we have in the past.

Catherine explains that many topics that are discussed openly now were rarely talked about in the past. Talking about our differences can be difficult, especially when we are worried about what others think and how they might react to us, but can help greatly with building confidence, acceptance, and self-belief.

Catherine says, "I think times are changing in a positive direction. At STAMMA we love seeing TikTok videos showing younger people talking about their stammering and being proud to speak whether they stammer or not."

Following our instincts

The more we tell those we trust about what makes us different, the more they can help us if we need it. Of course this can feel terrifying. We must follow our instincts about who are "safe" people to talk to, seeking out the best sources of kindness and support. As well as adults, we can find our own tribe of friends and decide when the right time is to confide in them.

If we take care of ourselves, we can open up to others at exactly the right time for us.

Some Questions for You to Answer

Key Question: Why is this book important?

....

....

....

....

Key Question: Has this book made you feel differently about yourself?

....

....

....

....

Key Question: Is there anyone you will treat differently now?

....

....

....

Key Question: "We are all normal. We just have different differences," says Afua. Do you think she's right, and why?

....

....

....

....

Key Question: "Everyone has something different about them," says Luna. If she's right, why is that important?

....

....

....

....

Advice from Someone a Bit Older Than You

At 16, Uriella, from Virginia, USA, who has epilepsy, has spent some years teaching herself how to build her confidence in difficult situations. Here are some of her suggestions.

ADVICE FROM SOMEONE A BIT OLDER THAN YOU

1. **Don't act like a victim**
   If you do, you will most likely be an easy target and feel uncomfortable. My goal is to stand up for myself, even if it gets me into trouble.

2. **Explain yourself to others**
   If others are giving you a hard time, this means either they don't understand you or they don't care. In other words, they don't deserve to be friends with you. Explain your situation to them. If they still don't care, 100% they don't deserve you.

   I've realized I need to explain about having epilepsy to people at my school: what it means and what it's like, as this will help other people understand me better. I made a video to show all of this because I didn't want people to feel alarmed if they saw me having a seizure and I wanted them to know what to do to help. For instance I wanted them to know that I feel fine after a seizure, and they only need to call the emergency services if I have been unconscious for more than five minutes or have lost a lot of blood.

   I also organized the Purple Pumpkin Project at my school, to spread awareness of epilepsy. I ask anyone who wanted to take part to decorate a pumpkin in purple, the "epilepsy colour".

3. **Make your voice heard**
   If someone's helping me and I ask them to stop so I can be independent, and they don't, I feel

uncomfortable and ignored. This has taught me that if I'm not heard the first time, I need to speak up to make sure people listen.

4. **Don't let people get in your way**
   This doesn't mean copying someone's bullying or thoughtless behaviour. There are other ways. Use a tone that's firm, not mean. Find your normal voice and, if they don't listen, speak up.

5. **Never forget that saying no might sound negative, but it can be positive**
   Saying no to others can be a way of saying yes to yourself. Stick to your guns until your message comes across.

6. **Try not to compare yourself with others**
   Be kind to yourself about who you are and challenge any thoughts that aren't sympathetic and caring. Take your concerns seriously and discuss them with someone you trust. You are worth every moment.

A Chat with One Parent

I spoke to Emma, a parent of one of the children in this book. She told me why she thinks we need to be more open-minded about all our differences.

Why do you feel so strongly about how children are treated who are different in some way?
Too often there are problems because society doesn't welcome and adapt to diversity as much as it should. Unless they have an impact on our health and wellbeing, the differences themselves are not the problem. We should be changing society to include people with differences. We all need to have the right attitude to help everyone to participate equally.

What happened when your daughter was born?
When Alisa was born, we discovered she had an extra finger on her right hand. We were referred to the Hand Unit of the Great Ormond Street Hospital in London. I went along expecting to discuss any issues

with how her hand might function. Instead, a plastic surgeon explained how surgery could make her hand look "basically normal" with any difference "hardly noticeable".

I was told that there wasn't anything she wouldn't be able to do with her six-fingered hand. Yet, the expectation was that we would feel that the more "normal" she looked, the better, and that we would want to have our toddler's unusual finger amputated for fear of her being bullied in later life.

You were shocked by this advice?
Well I really didn't want anything changed about my daughter. But I also asked myself, "What kind of message would we be giving her if she grew up knowing that her parents had put her through surgery to look 'more normal'?" I was worried it could encourage beliefs that you have to change to be accepted, that you should hide things about yourself in case others don't like them, or that you must sacrifice parts of yourself to be like the majority.

These were not messages I would ever want her to receive!

I also don't believe it is necessary to try to be as "normal" as possible in order to lead a full and happy life. In fact, the people I know who embrace their diversity are happier than the people I've seen trying to fit in. Our pharmacist has a double thumb on one hand,

and she said her parents had told her it was a sign of good luck. She said that when she faced name-calling at school, she saw this as something wrong with those who wanted to bully her, and her friends supported her. By the time she was an adult, she felt comfortable to be herself and pleased to have something so special about her.

Your pharmacist has a great attitude!

Yes, she does! We talked to her and lots of other people and we decided that Alisa must be allowed to decide for herself about her own body. We want to raise her with pride about all aspects of her identity, including her unusual hand. I felt encouraged to find an online group called the Lucky Fin Project with people who celebrate their hand differences. My hope is that society will take a firmer attitude to bullying based on any kind of difference, not just the well-known types. How much better it is for everyone when our children are accepted for exactly who they are!

A Few Ways Schools Can Help

> ❝When children feel that they're different, their voice can be powerful in helping others to understand that everybody is valuable in a school community, and everybody has something different to bring."

This is the view of Lisa Seddon, of Prescot Primary School in Merseyside, England. She says that in many schools, there's a culture of talking, communicating, and helping people to understand and support difference, including among children and young people themselves.

Here are some thoughts and ideas you could suggest to your school. These can help children and young teenagers have their say, educate their classmates, feel stronger, and grow in self-confidence.

The magic of one-on-one

In this book, so many children have talked about the importance of one-on-one time with someone they trust, to help them feel understood.

This individual attention gives children and young teens their own space in the crowded world of school. It's a time to be listened to without judgement, something we all need, no matter our age, explains Pip, a Pastoral Support Worker at a north London secondary school.

She says there's an advantage if the person you can talk to is someone who works at your school. You're in an environment that's familiar to you, with someone who knows you, and will also know anyone you have a problem with.

Tough times to be young

Pip believes it's never been as hard as it is now to be a young person. We are a much more open society than we used to be – we're no longer seen as odd if we're vegetarian, for example, as we were not very long ago – but we've created other problems, especially with online unpleasantness.

Along with the freedom to be different often comes the potential to be hurt and treated badly by others. There's an answer: "Giving someone who needs it the chance to be listened to and valued can help empower them. It's a human instinct," she says.

School can feel tough at times, but Pip points out our time in education is actually very short, if you think about how long a whole life can be.

A positive future

And there are always positives. "Difficulties we go through make us more rounded and empathetic as people," she says. "I am optimistic for the kids I work with. I do think life gets better. However bad they feel now, the sun will come out again."

Guest speakers

Prescot Primary has a slot in its assembly called "Guest Speakers". The speaker can be anyone, including children or staff who want to talk about a difference in their lives at a school assembly, anything from a medical condition to their country of origin. "The parents think it's fantastic that their children have the confidence to talk in front of everybody," says Lisa Seddon.

Different door

Another idea at Prescot Primary – a separate entrance for anyone having a rough start to their day. This is an option for them at any point in their school life. "If they go through that door, they get an individual welcome," says Lisa Seddon. "It's more of a one-to-one conversation with a member of staff. Maybe they'll have a piece of toast, maybe they'll have a cup of milk or something that just enables them to go, 'Right, OK, I'm in school. It's not so bad? Whatever issue they brought with them, they can talk about it and get to class by 9 o'clock and be ready to learn."

A special room

As Saphia mentions in her story, her high school has set up a room called The Hub for anyone who needs a bit of a break. She describes it as "a quiet space with a beanbag and a table, and you can work or just sit". Sienna, in her story, says there's something slightly different in her school, a sensory room – a place to settle and be calm.

Lunchtime groups

Four of the contributors, Frida, Gracie, Luna, and T, talk about finding these groups valuable. For those who attend, they can be a source of friendship and understanding.

A book of your own

The Neurodivergent and Reading Specialist at Fusion Academy, Loudoun, in the USA, Nancy Knor, works one-on-one with children who haven't thrived in other school settings due to dyslexia.

One of her concerns is that her students seem not to understand what dyslexia is, causing them pain and confusion. She assigns her students a research project where they learn about the challenges and gifts associated with the way their brains are wired.

To help raise awareness and promote understanding, Nancy and her students have written **The Dyslexic Fiddler Crab: A Survival Guide for Kids with Dyslexia**. This is a dyslexia-friendly book with accessible read-aloud options, that uses the concept of the dyslexic fiddler crab – a crab with one huge claw and one little claw.

Nancy writes about the "huge claw strengths" and "little claw challenges" associated with dyslexia. It includes easy-to-understand explanations and first person accounts from some of her middle and high school students. The book's aim is to inspire other struggling learners aged 11–17, allowing them to survive and to thrive at school.

To see videos of Nancy's students, purchase **The Dyslexic Fiddler Crab** book, or share you own dyslexic story, visit www.thedyslexicfiddlercrab.com.

Simple ways to ask for help

At St Mary's School, Levenshulme, England, one of their tools is "Gimme 5" – a handprint where they can write their name and their teacher will come to them for a chat at some point in the day. Another is Chat Zone, a drop-in area for anyone with a concern or worry, available every lunchtime and run by a play therapist or pastoral lead, complete with emoji cushions. Everyone loves the cushions!

Messy play

St Mary's runs a special messy play group, involving water, sand, jelly, Playdough, and other messy things. It's a great way to help children feel calm and build confidence, bringing about long-term change and security.

Help with transition to high school

St Mary's runs an extended programme for pupils with additional needs, sometimes taking them on the bus to plan the route to high school and begin to develop independence. There's also an anti-bullying programme for the whole year, exploring the shift from one school to the next.

Using the curriculum

Teachers can actively look to seek opportunities to include texts and stories about significant people who reflect the make up of their class or school, in order to celebrate and normalize diversity. This is one way to include as many positive role models as possible.

Helping temporary teachers to do a good job

Helping supply teachers understand the children in their class is seen as important by some of the children in this book. St Mary's briefs staff when they arrive, and has background information on the children in their classes waiting for them.

Diversity days

As Lorcan suggests in his story, it's great when schools celebrate different diversity days. This can even be part of PE, when children can experience football for the visually impaired by using a ball with a bell inside it. External speakers, talks about issues such as ADHD and autism, and celebrations of food and other aspects of culture are all enriching.

Resources available for all

Some schools make resources for children with dyslexia, for instance coloured paper to read and write from, available for anyone who wants to use them. Ear defenders can also be left in a big box so anyone can grab some if they need them.

The No Outsiders Programme

All sorts of useful information is on this website, www.no-outsiders.com, including great ideas for assemblies, films, picture books, and lesson plans, plus a plaque to go outside your school gates, to help your school include everyone.

Key Question: How would you like your school to support its children who are different? Could you make some suggestions to your teachers?

Just Some of the Many Places Where You Can Go for Support

The charities and organizations below all help children. Some of them helped create this book, by finding amazing young people who wanted to be included. If these aren't local to you, you'll be able to find some that are. An extended version of this chapter can be found at: www.jkp.com/catalogue/book/9781805012924

Action Deaf Youth, Belfast
Action Deaf Youth (ADY) supports deaf children and young people all over Northern Ireland. It has a largely Deaf team of staff, offering support with language and communication, social needs, educational opportunities and navigating hearing-oriented society.

There are weekly group play sessions for children up to 11, youth sessions, residentials, summer schemes, family days, parent-child support programmes, and British Sign Language courses.

www.actiondeafyouth.org

A Kid Again
When children and teenagers go to the hospital or doctor's office because of life-threatening medical conditions, this can be scary.

A Kid Again provides time out from the difficult times, with year-round events including trips to theme parks, sports stadiums, and museums, all over the USA. These are a cost-free, carefree break from medical visits, infusions, chemotherapy and other treatment. The charity enables children and their siblings to develop new memories and friendships, and create a supportive network, in person and in online meetings.

www.akidagain.org

Cancer Fight Foundation
Cancer Fight Foundation is based in Kolkata, India. It helps those with cancer who have low income levels. Its focus is to help paediatric cancer patients and their families during and after their treatment. This includes counselling, nutritional advice, teaching, helping with extracurricular activities such as dance, singing and yoga, and providing educational support once treatment is over. Hundreds of children have been helped in a country where cancer has a large stigma attached to it.

www.cancerfightfoundation.com

Changing Faces
Changing Faces supports anyone in the UK with a scar, mark, or condition on their face or body that makes them look different. Its aim is to ensure that those they work with feel supported and accepted, no matter their age or background.

The charity helps young people build their confidence and learn how to handle people's reactions. It includes a wellbeing service, which include one-to-one counselling and workshops and online information. It offers somewhere to talk openly about feelings and learn more about life with a visible difference. Changing Faces also has resources which can be used by your school.

www.changingfaces.org.uk

Child Bereavement Center
This organization in the USA provides child and teen peer support groups, events, and resources.

www.childbereavement.org

JUST SOME OF THE MANY PLACES WHERE YOU CAN GO FOR SUPPORT

Child Bereavement UK

Child Bereavement UK helps children and young people when someone important to them is dying or has died. They give support either face-to-face or by telephone, online, or instant messenger. The organization also runs groups where bereaved young people can meet others with similar experiences for social activities and to work together on creative projects.

www.childbereavementuk.org

Children Heard and Seen

Children Heard and Seen supports children and young people with a parent in prison. The children are, of course, completely innocent, yet often experience feelings of shame and stigma because of their parent's offending. The organization's support includes one-to-one sessions in their local community with a trained practitioner, a space to process difficult emotions. It also offers group activities, where children can make connections with others who share their experiences.

www.childrenheardandseen.co.uk

Diabetes UK

This organization supports people in the UK living with all types of diabetes, as well as those at risk of type 2 diabetes. It campaigns to change policies and attitudes towards diabetes, changes lives through ground-breaking research, and provides information, support, and advice to those who need it.

Children and young people can find support through Diabetes UK by attending one of their Type 1 events for children and families, or through the Together Type 1 programme, a community for young people aged 11–25. This brings together people who understand what it's like, juggling the ups and downs of life with diabetes.

www.diabetes.org.uk

Epilepsy Action

Epilepsy Action has resources on its website to help children and parents deal with an epilepsy diagnosis. Some of its information is tailored for children aged 5–11 to understand and for them to realize they aren't alone, encouraging them to feel more confident. The organization also offers local and online Talk and

Support groups for parents of children with epilepsy so they can meet others with similar experiences.

www.epilepsy.org.uk (with an online Live Chat)

Epilepsy Foundation
This runs a Kids Crew to help children with epilepsy in the USA. It includes education materials, a summer camp, and a helpline.

www.epilepsy.com

Facing the World
Facing the World runs centres of excellence in the countries where it works to provide surgery to children with disabling facial differences.

www.facingtheworld.net

Family Carers Ireland
This organization provides individual support for any young carer struggling with their lives in any way. It provides information, advice, practical support, and counselling and explains how to plan for emergencies. It also gives support to the wider family.

Young carers meet each other and learn from each other, gaining important emotional support. A Young Carers Card guarantees free entry to lots of fun activities. An annual Young Carers Respite weekend allows young carers to meet and have fun, and conferences allow them to have their voices heard. Groups run by therapists tackle issues including mental health, isolation, stress, and bullying as well as study skills.

https://familycarers.ie/carer-supports/young-carers
Freephone Careline: 1800 240724

Guide Dogs
Guide Dogs operates a wide range of services in the UK, to support people living with a vision impairment, with and without dogs. It works with children, adults, friends, and family to help people with sight loss live well and independently.

This is the largest employer of specialists dedicated to helping children and young people overcome the challenges of sight loss, including at their nurseries, schools, and colleges. It produces custom-made books, with font size, spacing, paper colour, and other details all tailored to suit a child's individual needs. Guide Dogs provides personalized advice on the best technology to support children's needs and provides the technology, devices, and software free of charge. It also hosts a UK-wide programme of family activity days.

www.guidedogs.org.uk/getting-support

IMIX

IMIX helps those with experience of migration to express themselves and tell their stories, playing its part in increasing understanding about refugees and the experiences they face in their lives. By putting a human face on to complex issues, it aims to create greater understanding and empathy for those who have made the UK their home. Over time it builds confidence, thanks to in-depth support.

www.imix.org.uk

Malawi Girl Guides Association

The Malawi Girl Guides Association helps girls and young women in Malawi to reach their full potential. It welcomes girls who are in school and out of school, those with HIV, special needs, disabilities, teenage mothers, and all others.

It teaches life skills and leadership training. It empowers girls and young women to take part in decision-making at all levels in what is often a male-dominated society. The organization helps develop entrepreneurial skills through working with local projects and emphasizes health and wellbeing issues, including helping their members to make their own sanitary towels. Activities include camping, dancing, sports, drama, and much more.

www.magga.mw

Mind Monsters

Julie Derrick has published two children's books to help younger children deal with Obsessive Compulsive Disorder, or OCD – see www.childhoodocd.co.uk.

These books introduce examples of OCD themes and triggers and provide strategies to help children start speaking up about OCD.

She has also created a digital **Parenting OCD in Teens and Tweens** handbook that helps parents support teenagers with OCD while they wait for professional therapy.

www.childhoodocd.co.uk

MIRA USA/MIRA Canada

This charity helps empower and improve the quality of life for blind children, including providing guide dogs.

www.mirausa.org
www.mira.ca

PC Project

PC stands for Pachyonychia Congenita – see Cora's story in this book. The PC Project offers support to patients in more than 50 countries.

As well as seeking a cure, PC Project holds patient support meetings and online forums where patients can meet others who experience the same difficulties. They learn they are not alone and find effective ways to cope while focusing on their strengths and special gifts and talents.

www.pachyonychia.org

Refugee Education UK

Refugee Education UK works alongside refugee and asylum-seeking young people, supporting them to gain access to and thrive in education in the UK, from primary school all the way to university. The charity organizes education support programmes for young people and training programmes for people working in education. Its work is aimed at helping educational environments to become places where young refugees are welcomed and able to thrive.

www.reuk.org

Scottish Association for Children with Heart Disorders

SACHD provides support to children, young people, and their families. It organizes parties at Easter, Halloween and Christmas for children and their families, plus annual weekends in Pitlochry for families.

It has a teen support group for those from 12–19. This includes days out and annual teen weekends away, solely for those with heart disorders. The charity organizes events to provide peer support, increase confidence, and boost self-esteem within the group.

www.youngheart.info

Sickle Cell Society

The Sickle Cell Society is the only national charity in the UK that supports and represents people affected by a sickle cell disorder to improve their overall quality of life. The Society's aim is to empower them to achieve their full potential while managing the challenges they face. It has a national helpline and online service and organizes children's activities and an annual holiday. The children benefit from educational and social support, and peer mentoring.

www.sicklecellsociety.org

Sightsavers

Sightsavers protects sight, fights disease, and helps make sure people with disabilities can claim their rights. The organization works in more than 30 low- and middle-income countries in Africa and Asia. In schools, Sightsavers trains teachers to help students with disabilities learn and reach their potential. It also supports children who need glasses or learning equipment and helps governments make sure their education systems include everyone.

www.sightsavers.org

STAMMA

STAMMA is also known as the British Stammering Association and its website provides information on all aspects of stammering, therapy options, and how to find support, plus people's stories and useful videos. It runs parent workshops and support groups and a Minecraft club for children aged 7–14. The charity also hosts a regular family day for young people and their families to get together in person. STAMMA has created a community for people of all ages to have their voices heard.

www.stamma.org

Tourettes Action

Anyone with Tourette's can contact Tourettes Action for friendship and support. One of its main goals is to provide support and training within schools and advocate for students there, making the educational journey as smooth as possible.

Tourettes Action runs weekend residential events throughout the year. At these, those with Tourette's and their families can build personal confidence, resilience, and a sense of community.

The charity has a helpdesk for anyone in need of help and holds conferences, workshops, meetings and seminars on topics of interest.

Online support groups bring together those wanting to connect with others in their situation. There are other fun activities and face-to-face support groups across the country, helping to build confidence and friendships.

www.tourettes-action.org.uk

Books You May Like

FOR TEACHERS
Square Pegs: Inclusivity, Compassion and Fitting In. A Guide for Schools by Fran Morgan with Ellie Costello, edited by Ian Gilbert

FOR YOUNG CHILDREN
It's OK To Be Different by Sharon Purtill
Just Ask. Be Different, Be Brave, Be You by Sonia Sotomayor
Not Like the Others by Dr Jana Broecker
Just Like Me by Louise Gooding

THE BOOK MENTIONED BY OLIVIA AND ALISA
Wonder by RJ Palacio

ANOTHER LOVELY BOOK ABOUT DIFFERENCE
The Boy at the Back of the Class by Onjali Rauf

Acknowledgements

Thanks to all the fantastic children and young teens who spoke to me for this book. It's been great to talk to you and hear all about your lives. I learnt so much from all of you. Thanks too to the schools, charities, parents, and others who have helped me find you!

Thank you to Jessica Kingsley Publishers, especially Amy Lankester-Owen, her colleagues, and the production team. Kudos to the sales team – thanks for your support for all of my books. Special thanks to Abbie Howard.

Big thanks as always to my lovely family and to my agent and sounding-board Jane Judd. Thanks to wordsmiths Claire Armitstead and Sarah Neville. Thanks to everyone who has helped me develop my book writing, with a special mention for Frances Dunne who sat across from me in a café ten years ago and said, "I know you can do this."

With Thanks to...

A Kid Again and Ann Fixari

Action Deaf Youth, Belfast and Julie Graham

Anne Metcalfe

Changing Faces and Shelley Ruffles

Child Bereavement UK and Jane Nattras

Children Heard and Seen – Sarah Burrows and Felix Tasker

Christine Nicholls

Connor Magennis

Courtney Rivard, The Magic Foundation

Diabetes UK – Helen Riley and Jon Matthias

Donna Colbourne

Epilepsy Action – Rebecca and Giada

Evelyn Magennis

Family Carers Ireland and Catherine Cox

Fergus Magennis

Guide Dogs and Paul Martin

Hannah Oakley

IMIX and Katie Bryson

Jen Thomas

Kate McGeever

Lawnswood School and Anna Mason

Linda Bannister

Linda Martin

Liz Barron

Magic Foundation and Courtney Rivard

Malawi Girl Guides Association – Tamanda Mlumbe and Jim Dyson

Marcia Brissett-Bailey

Mind Monsters and Julie Derrick

Molly Holding

Nancy Knor

Nick Hardwick

PC Project and Janice Schwartz

Prescot Primary School and Lisa Seddon

Prison Advice & Care Trust

Refugee Education UK – Niwaeli Sumary and Moses Seitler

Rimi Ananya Mukherjee-Mehra, Co-founder of the Cancer Fight Foundation

RNID and Dawn Dimond

Saffron Cooksey

Sarah Hymas

Schools of Sanctuary

Scottish Association for Children with Heart Disorders and Lesley Kinnear

Sickle Cell Society and Keyah Miller

Sightsavers

Skin Care Cymru and Dr Julie Peconi

Slievemore Clinic, especially Rebecca

St Anne's Primary School, Knowsley, and Linda Bannister

St Joseph the Worker School, Kirkby, and Shell Sisk

St Mary's, Levenshulme, especially Mylene McGuire and Joanne O'Mullane

STAMMA – Jane Powell and Neha Shaji

Stoke Newington School, especially Pip Ainsworth, Alex Bell, Leila Alkunshalie

Taylor Richardson

Tourettes Action and Emma McNally

FINAL WORD FROM CONNOR, 12:

"We must keep trying, keep pushing, do the same thing we're doing. We must make sure we're around people we want to be around, to have a good environment around us, to build the best lives we can. That's what we can do – that and never give up!"

by the same author

You Can Change the World
Everyday Heroes Making a Difference Everywhere
Margaret Rooke
Forewords by Taylor Richardson and Kate Hodgetts
ISBN 978 1 78592 502 3
eISBN 978 1 78450 897 5

Meet the Dyslexia Club
The Amazing Talents, Skills and Everyday
Life of Children with Dyslexia
Margaret Rooke
Illustrated by Tim Stringer
Foreword by Róisín Lowe
ISBN 978 1 83997 843 2
eISBN 978 1 83997 844 9

Dyslexia is My Superpower (Most of the Time)
Margaret Rooke
Forewords by Catherine Drennan and Loyle Carner
ISBN 978 1 78592 299 2
eISBN 978 1 78450 606 3